# An Age of Voyages
# 1350-1600

## Teaching Guide

Oxford University Press, Inc., publishes works that
further Oxford University's objective of excellence
in research, scholarship, and education.

Oxford   New York
Auckland   Cape Town   Dar es Salaam   Hong Kong   Karachi
Kuala Lumpur   Madrid   Melbourne   Mexico City   Nairobi
New Delhi   Shanghai   Taipei   Toronto

With offices in
Argentina   Austria   Brazil   Chile   Czech Republic   France   Greece
Guatemala   Hungary   Italy   Japan Poland   Portugal   Singapore
South Korea   Switzerland   Thailand   Turkey   Ukraine   Vietnam

Copyright © 2005 by Oxford University Press, Inc.

Published by Oxford University Press, Inc.
198 Madison Avenue, New York, NY, 10016
www.oup.com

Oxford is a registered trademark of Oxford University Press

All rights reserved.  No part of this publication may be reproduced,
stored in a retrieval system, or transmitted, in any form or by any means,
electronic, mechanical, photocopying, recording, or otherwise,
without the prior permission of Oxford University Press.

ISBN-13: 978-0-19-522253-1 (California edition)   ISBN-13: 978-0-19-522344-6

Project Director: Jacqueline A. Ball
Education Consultant: Diane L Brooks, Ed.D.
Editors: Georgia Scurletis, Katherine Schulten
Design: dlabnyc

Casper Grathwohl, Publisher

Printed in the United States of America
on acid-free paper

# AN AGE OF VOYAGES, 1350–1600 MOVIES AND DOCUMENTARIES

Consider using the following films, videos, and DVDs to stimulate student interest in this historical period, or for extension and enrichment. Teachers should preview all films and be aware that like historical fiction, films are not always accurate in details.

***The Black Death*** (1995). From Transatlantic Films *History's Turning Point* series. With dramatizations carried out at the actual sites of the events, this series has been highly praised as a motivating addition to secondary and college classes. Includes a Teacher's Guide.

***The Black Death*** (Interactive). From the Discovery Channel website: *http://media.dsc.discovery.com/anthology/momentsintime/blackdeath/blackdeath.html*.

***Christianity: The First Two Thousand Years*** (2001). A 2-disc DVD set from A&E with a standard full-frame transfer and Dolby Digital Stereo sound. Closed captions are accessible. Disc 1 contains *The First Thousand Years* and Disc 2 contains *The Second Thousand Years*. The set also includes a historical millennium timeline.

***Elizabeth*** (2002). An informative 2-volume DVD release from A&E that reveals almost everything one would want to know about the life of Queen Elizabeth.

***Hamlet*** Of the many film versions of Shakespeare's tragedy, Laurence Olivier's *Hamlet* (1948) is probably the most noteworthy. You may also wish to see Kevin Kline's *Hamlet* (1990). This adaptation of *Hamlet* was originally produced for PBS, where it first aired in 1990. Both versions are available on VHS and DVD.

***Legends of Monkey King*** (2002). The classic Chinese story *The Journey to the West* has been translated into English in this animated video.

***The Lost Empire*** (2001), directed by Peter MacDonald, is in many respects a sequel to the original *Journey to the West*, as opposed to being a modern rendition of the original story.

***Man of La Mancha*** (1973). Directed by Arthur Hiller and featuring Peter O'Toole and Sophia Loren; this film is available on DVD and VHS from Warner Home Video.

***Martin Luther*** (1953). Irving Pichel's film is available on VHS and DVD. This is the story of Luther's efforts to reform the Catholic Church, his excommunication, and the developments that led to the Protestant Reformation.

***Suleyman the Magnificent*** (1986). A documentary shot on location in Istanbul, Edirne, and the Turkish countryside, it explores the political, social, and cultural background of the Ottoman Empire during the reign of Sultan Suleyman (1520–1566).

# CONTENTS

| | |
|---|---|
| Note to the Teacher | 5 |
| *The Medieval & Early Modern World* Program<br>Using the Teaching Guide and Student Study Guide | 6 |
| Improving Literacy with *The Medieval & Early Modern World* | 16 |
| Group Projects | 20 |
| Teaching Strategies for *An Age of Voyages, 1350–1600* | |
| Chapter 1  Disease and Disaster: The Dreadful 14th Century | 26 |
| Chapter 2  Renaissance Men and Renaissance Money:<br>Learning and Art in Italy and Beyond | 32 |
| Chapter 3  Ghosts, Monkeys, or Confucius: Learning as Power in Ming China | 38 |
| Chapter 4  Black and White and Read All Over: The Printing Press | 44 |
| Chapter 5  Luther, Loyola, Mobs, and Massacres:<br>The Protestant and Catholic Reformations | 50 |
| Chapter 6  "Astonishing," "Magnificent," "Great":<br>Rulers and Religion in Europe and Asia | 56 |
| Chapter 7  Guts, Gain, and Glory: Powerful Monarchs in England and Africa | 62 |
| Chapter 8  "Everything the World Has to Offer": City Life | 68 |
| Chapter 9  Silk and Spices: Travel and Trade in the Mediterranean Sea<br>and the Indian Ocean | 74 |
| Chapter 10  "Columbia" or "America"? Names and Fame in a "New World" | 80 |
| Chapter 11  Sailors, Sugar, and Slaves:<br>How European Voyages Changed Asia and Africa | 86 |
| Chapter 12  Germs, Silver, and Blood:<br>New World Conquests and Global Connections | 92 |
| Wrap-Up Test | 98 |
| Rubrics | 100 |
| Graphic Organizers | 104 |
| Answer Key (Teaching Guide and Student Study Guide) | 112 |

# HISTORY FROM OXFORD UNIVERSITY PRESS

"A thoroughly researched political and cultural history... makes for a solid resource for any collection."
– School Library Journal

**THE WORLD IN ANCIENT TIMES**
RONALD MELLOR AND AMANDA H. PODANY, EDS.
THE EARLY HUMAN WORLD
THE ANCIENT NEAR EASTERN WORLD
THE ANCIENT EGYPTIAN WORLD
THE ANCIENT SOUTH ASIAN WORLD
THE ANCIENT CHINESE WORLD
THE ANCIENT GREEK WORLD
THE ANCIENT ROMAN WORLD
THE ANCIENT AMERICAN WORLD

"Bringing history out of the Dark Ages!"

**THE MEDIEVAL AND EARLY MODERN WORLD**
BONNIE G. SMITH, ED.
THE EUROPEAN WORLD, 400-1450
THE AFRICAN AND MIDDLE EASTERN WORLD, 600-1500
THE ASIAN WORLD, 600-1500
AN AGE OF EMPIRES, 1200-1750
AN AGE OF VOYAGES, 1350-1600
AN AGE OF SCIENCE AND REVOLUTIONS, 1600-1800

"The liveliest, most realistic, most well-received American history series ever written for children."
– Los Angeles Times

**A HISTORY OF US**
JOY HAKIM
THE FIRST AMERICANS
MAKING THIRTEEEN COLONIES
FROM COLONIES TO COUNTRY
THE NEW NATION
LIBERTY FOR ALL?
WAR, TERRIBLE WAR
RECONSTRUCTING AMERICA
AN AGE OF EXTREMES
WAR, PEACE, AND ALL THAT JAZZ
ALL THE PEOPLE

FOR MORE INFORMATION, VISIT US AT WWW.OUP.COM

New from Oxford University Press
Reading History, by Janet Allen
ISBN 0-19-516595-0 hc  0-19-516596-9 pb

"*Reading History* is a great idea. I highly recommend this book."
–Dennis Denenberg, *Professor of Elementary and Early Childhood Education, Millersville University*

# NOTE TO THE TEACHER

Dear Fellow Educator:

How do we realize our hopes and dreams? How do we face the challenges of everyday life? Everyone—old and young alike—asks such questions at one time or another. One place to look for answers is in the lives of people in the past. In history we find ordinary people building cathedrals and mosques, conducting trade over thousands of miles, eking out a living through agriculture and crafts, and dreaming dreams of creating vast empires. This series brings you their stories.

As educators, we want to present these stories as part of a living past—and the authors of our books aim to provide you with the materials to do just that. We offer ways to make the past come alive with vivid images in full color, lively accounts of actual people, and maps to show young readers where these people lived and how they traveled the world. Heroes tell us in their own words of their noblest hopes; villains show us their cruelty. Ordinary folks face the plague and young boys set out in creaky ships on dangerous seas. This series helps you show young adults the fullness of the past and the grand achievements that make up our heritage.

We all know that our task does not stop at presenting the *story* of the past. We must also teach our students the *skills* vital to understanding history and to becoming informed citizens. These books are designed to help you train students to think critically about human opinions, prejudices, and programs for the future. The many voices from historical actors in the series provide opportunities for students to come to terms with burning issues of bias and point of view.

You and I share not only great hopes for the future but also the daily challenges of teaching. In addition to the stories, images, quotes, maps, timelines, and young adult bibliographies of the books themselves, the series includes instructional guides with tested ideas for teaching the medieval and early modern world. These guides are filled with exercises, classroom activities, and daily lessons based on specific chapters in each book. They show additional, practical ways to make critical thinking an integral part of your work in world history.

The authors of the student books and the supporting instructional materials bring you and your students the very latest thinking about what world history is. We urge you to tell us how their presentation of this vital, emerging field works with your students. Good history, like the creation of civilization itself, depends on our common effort!

Bonnie G. Smith
*General Editor*

# THE MEDIEVAL & EARLY MODERN WORLD PROGRAM

### I. STUDENT EDITION

- Engaging, friendly narrative
- A wide range of primary sources in every chapter
- The authority of Oxford scholarship
- Period illustrations and specially commissioned maps

### II. TEACHING GUIDE

- Wide range of activities and classroom approaches
- Strategies for universal access and improving literacy (ELL, struggling readers, advanced learners)
- Multiple assessment tools

### III. STUDENT STUDY GUIDE

- Exercises correlated to Student Edition and Teaching Guide
- Portfolio approach
- Activities for every level of learning
- Literacy through reading and writing

### PRIMARY SOURCES AND REFERENCE VOLUME

- Broad selection of primary sources in each subject area
- Ideal resource for in-class exercises and unit projects

# TEACHING GUIDE: KEY FEATURES

The Teaching Guides organize each *Medieval & Early Modern World* book into chapter-based lessons of six (6) pages each, preceded by a special section that includes one longer-term project per chapter. These projects are cross-curricular, designed for mixed-group participation, and suitable for a wide range of learning styles. They can be used for teacher and student self- or peer assessment with the rubrics at the back of this Teaching Guide.

## GROUP PROJECTS
Engaging, creative projects for group work on a wide variety of inviting topics

## CHAPTER LESSONS
Teaching strategies and suggestions that address curriculum and that link with Student Study Guide and Student Edition

## TESTS AND BLACKLINE MASTERS (BLMS)
Reproducible tests; map skills, primary sources, and document-based questions (DBQs) for assessment, homework, or classroom projects

# TEACHING GUIDE: CHAPTER LESSONS

Teaching guides are organized so that you can easily find the information you need.

**CHAPTER SUMMARY AND PERFORMANCE OBJECTIVES**
The Chapter Summary gives an overview of the information in the chapter. The Performance Objectives are the three or four important goals students should achieve in the chapter. Accomplishing these goals will help students master the information in the book as well as meet standards for the course.

**BUILDING BACKGROUND**
This section connects students to the chapter they are about to read. Students may be asked to use what they know to make predictions about the text, preview the images in the chapter, or connect modern life with the historical subject matter.

**VOCABULARY**
A word list for every chapter defines difficult words and key curricular terms and recaps glossary entries.

### CHAPTER 1
### BELIEVERS AND BARBARIANS: THE END OF THE ROMAN EMPIRE
PAGES 20–33

FOR HOMEWORK
Student Study Guide pages
Chapter 1    13–16

**CHAPTER SUMMARY**
Both external and internal problems weakened Rome. When Constantine the Great converted to Christianity he moved the capital east to a city later renamed Constantinople. The empire gradually divided into the Eastern Empire and the Western Empire, each with its own version of Christianity. In 410 the Visigoths conquered Rome. However, Rome's legacy lived on through Latin, government structures, and architecture.

**PERFORMANCE OBJECTIVES**
▶ To identify the factors that threatened the Roman Empire
▶ To define and evaluate the key events in the life and rule of Constantine
▶ To identify the lasting contributions of Rome

**BUILDING BACKGROUND**
Ask students to preview the chapter by reading the headings and subheadings, studying the photographs and captions, and examining the map. Based on the preview, work with students to compile a list of questions about the fall of Rome and the rise of Christianity. As students locate the answers to their questions, have them record them on the list.

**VOCABULARY**
**empire** huge region of varied cultures under the control of one government
**citizen** person owing loyalty to and entitled to protection by a state or a nation
**Christianity** the religion based on the life and teachings of Jesus Christ
**convert** person who has been convinced to change from one religion to another
**barbarian** name given to outsiders by the Romans, who viewed them as uncivilized
**drought** a long period of very low rainfall
As needed, have students consult the glossary to define the following words: *bishop, centralize, council, excommunicate, heretic, New Testament, persecution, plunder, saint*

**CAST OF CHARACTERS**
**Augustine** (aw-GUS-teen), Roman nobleman who converted to Christianity
**Constantine the Great** (KON-stun-teen), First Roman emperor to convert to Christianity
**Visigoths** (VIH-zih-goths), Arian Christian Germanic tribe that attacked Rome in 410

**WORKING WITH PRIMARY SOURCES**
Point out the quotation from Ambrose in Student Edition page 23. If necessary, refer students to the glossary, and explain that excommunicated means to be deprived of the right of church membership by the church leadership. Discuss what the quotation reveals about early Christian beliefs. Why do you think Ambrose asked the emperor to repent? Invite students to read more of Ambrose's letter to the emperor, written in 390, at http://www.fordham.edu/halsall/source/ambrose-let51.html.

28 CHAPTER 1

**WORKING WITH PRIMARY SOURCES**
A major feature of *The Medieval & Early Modern World* is the opportunity to read about history through the words and images of the people who lived it. Each book includes excerpts from the best sources from these ancient civilizations, giving the narrative an immediacy that is difficult to match in secondary sources. Students can read further in these sources on their own or in small groups using the accompanying *Primary Sources and Reference Volume*. The Teaching Guide recommends activities so students of all skill levels can appreciate the ways people from the past saw themselves, their ideas and values, and their fears and dreams.

**LINKING DISCIPLINES**

**Art** Have students research examples of arches, roads, and aqueducts constructed throughout the Roman Empire. You might want to display a map of the Roman Empire on the wall. Instruct students to research in a library or on the Internet to find examples of Roman architecture. Have them sketch or print copies, write brief captions, and affix them on the map. Ask students to identify similarities between these ancient structures and familiar modern structures.

**LITERACY TIPS**

In addition to using the suggestions in the Supporting Learning and Extending Learning sections, refer back to pages 20–23 for strategies and advice from a literacy coach.

### WRITING

**Persuasive Letter** Have students review the events of Augustine's life as described in the chapter. Next have them write a persuasive letter or sermon that he might have addressed to non-Christians to describe his conversion and persuade them of his beliefs. What figurative language might he use to compel them? What experiences would he share from his life? (*Assessment: students incorporate supporting detail and language from the chapter. Their letters should also represent the tensions between Christians and non-Christians.*)

### SUPPORTING LEARNING

**English Language Learners** Help students recognize and use multiple-meaning words. Using the paragraphs on Student Edition page 27, identify and define such words as letters, beat, torn, and passage. Help students use context clues and their prior knowledge to figure out which meaning is being used. Ask volunteers to suggest sentences using various meanings of the words.

**Struggling Readers** Have students complete the Sequence of Events Chart at the back of the guide to show how one event led to another, and then another, in the history of early Christianity. For example, they can list how Christianity's spread led to the executions of Christians, and so on. Remind them to look for key dates, such as Constantine's conversion in 312.

### EXTENDING LEARNING

**Enrichment** Invite students to learn more about one of these cities as they are today: Rome, Carthage, or Constantinople. Direct students to search engines, or to consult websites such as...

### GEOGRAPHY CONNECTION

**Movement** Have students trace the routes of the Germanic migrations on the map on page 31. They may want to compare the map with a topographic map of Europe to locate features, such as mountains or rivers that either blocked or aided the movement of these peoples.

### READING COMPREHENSION QUESTIONS

1. Why did economic and social conditions worsen in Rome? (*Rome depended on slaves to produce food. When the empire stopped expanding, it had fewer slaves do the work.*)
2. Why did Roman authorities fear the early Christians? (*They worried about uprisings. Christianity was becoming popular among people who would likely rebel: the poor in cities, slaves, and soldiers.*)
3. Where did Constantine locate the new capital of the empire? (*Byzantium, a small Greek city near Asia Minor*)
4. Why did the Huns migrate west? (*Drought ruined their pasture, and they wanted better lives for themselves.*)
5. What happened after the Visigoths advanced on Rome in 410? (*The western emperor fled, and the Visigoths plundered Rome.*)

### CRITICAL THINKING QUESTIONS

1. What does the image of the shield on Student Edition page 23 tell you about warfare during this time? (*Warfare included hand-to-hand combat. Soldiers had access to iron for added protection.*)
2. Why were the Romans, Germanic tribes, and Huns in conflict with each other? (*They wanted to either keep control of land and resources, or gain land and resources from the other groups. They fought rather than cooperate with each other.*)
3. One Goth observer described the Huns as "small, foul, and skinny." What does it say about the Goths' view of the Huns during this time? (*It shows their negative opinion of the Goths.*)

### SOCIAL SCIENCES

**Military History** Attila the Hun is still famous today for his resilience and brutality. Have students research his attack on Rome using the Internet or library resources. Next have them use their history journals to write from Attila's point of view a series of short diary entries describing his advance toward Rome.

### READING AND LANGUAGE ARTS

**Reading Nonfiction** As students read the text, have them use the strategy "list/group/label" to work with the vocabulary. First have them individually list words that relate to different cultures or religious groups as they read. Then have students form groups of three and share their lists. Next, ask the groups to identify and name at least five categories in which to put the words, and sort them into the categories to which they best belong. Finally, have each small group display their choices and share the reasons behind them with the class.

**Using Language** Direct students' attention to the quotation from Ambrose on page 27. Have them draw in their history journals an image it brings to mind. With partners, students can share images and discuss what Ambrose might have described the church the way he did. Next, have partners consider what the "raging sea" represents. As a whole class, speculate about the effect of his words on both Christians and on non-Christians.

---

**WRITING**
Each chapter has a suggestion for a specific writing assignment. These assignments can help students meet state requirements in writing as well improve their skills.

**SUPPORTING LEARNING AND EXTENDING LEARNING**
Suggestions for students of varying abilities and learning styles: advanced learners, struggling readers, auditory/visual/tactile learners, and English language learners. These may be individual, partner, or group activities. (For more on reading and literacy, see pp. 16–19.)

**GEOGRAPHY CONNECTION**
Each chapter has a Geography Connection to strengthen students' map skills as well as their understanding of how geography affects human civilization. One of the five themes of geography is highlighted in each chapter.

**READING COMPREHENSION AND CRITICAL THINKING QUESTIONS**
The reading comprehension questions are general enough to allow free-flowing class or small group discussion, yet specific enough to be used for oral or written assessment of students' grasp of the important information. The critical thinking questions are intended to engage students in a deeper analysis of the text and can also be used for oral or written assessment.

**SOCIAL SCIENCES ACTIVITIES**
These activities connect the subject matter in the Student Edition with economics, civics, and science, technology, and society.

**READING AND LANGUAGE ARTS**
Some activities can facilitate the development of nonfiction reading strategies. Others help students' appreciation of fiction and poetry, focusing on word choice, description, and figurative language.

THE EUROPEAN WORLD, 400–1450

# TEACHING GUIDE: CHAPTER SIDEBARS

Icons quickly help identify key concepts, facts, activities, and assessment activities in the sidebars.

▶ **Cast of Characters**
This sidebar points out and identifies significant personalities in the chapter. Pronunciation guides are included where necessary.

▶ **Then and Now**
This feature provides interesting facts and ideas about the ancient civilization and relates it to the modern world. This may be an aspect of government still in use today, word origins of common modern expressions, physical reminders of the past, and other features. You can use this item simply to promote interest in the subject matter or as a springboard to other research.

▶ **Linking Disciplines**
This feature offers opportunities to investigate other subject areas that relate to the material in the Student Edition: math, science, arts, and health. Specific areas of these subjects are emphasized: **Math** (arithmetic, algebra, geometry, data, statistics); **Science** (life science, earth science, physical science); **Arts** (music, arts, dance, drama, architecture); **Health** (personal health, world health).

▶ **For Homework**
A quick glance links you to additional activities in the Student Study Guide that can be assigned as homework.

# ASSESSMENT

*The Medieval & Early Modern World* program intentionally omits from the Student Edition the kinds of section, chapter, and unit questions that are used to review and assess learning in standard textbooks. It is the purpose of the series to engage readers in learning—and loving—history written as good literature. Rather than interrupting student reading and enjoyment, all assessment instruments for the series have been placed in the Teaching Guides.

### ▶ CHAPTER TESTS
A reproducible chapter test follows each chapter in this Teaching Guide. These tests will help you assess students' mastery of the content addressed in each chapter. These tests measure a variety of cognitive and analytical skills, particularly comprehension, critical thinking, and expository writing through multiple choice, short answer, and essay questions.
*An answer key for the chapter tests is provided at the end of the Teaching Guide.*

### ▶ WRAP-UP TEST
After the last chapter test you will find a wrap-up test consisting of 10 essay questions that evaluate students' ability to synthesize and express what they've learned about the civilization under study. Depending upon your class, you may want to consider assigning the questions as a takehome or open-book test.

### ▶ RUBRICS
The rubrics at the back of this Teaching Guide will help you assess students' written work, oral presentations, and group projects. They include a Scoring Rubric based on standards for good writing and effective cooperative learning. In addition, a simplified hand-out is provided, plus a form for evaluating group projects and a Library/Media Center Research Log to help students focus and evaluate their research. Students can also evaluate their own work using these rubrics.

### ▶ BLACKLINE MASTERS (BLMs)
Two blackline masters follow each chapter in the Teaching Guide. These BLMs are reproducible pages for you to use as in-class activities or homework exercises. Assigning primary source blackline masters to groups or partners is strongly encouraged, as this material may be quite challenging to some students. They can also be used for assessment as needed.

### ▶ ADDITIONAL ASSESSMENT ACTIVITIES
The Group Project sections and Chapter Lessons of this Teaching Guide provide numerous activities and projects that have been designated as additional assessment opportunities, using the rubrics at the back of this Guide.

## USING THE STUDENT STUDY GUIDE FOR ASSESSMENT

▶ Study Guide Activities
Assignments in the Student Study Guide correspond with those in the Teaching Guide. If needed, these Student Study Guide activities can be used for assessment.

▶ Portfolio Approach
Student Study Guide pages can be removed from the workbook and turned in for grading. When the pages are returned, they can be part of the students' individual history journals. Have students keep a 3-ring binder portfolio of Study Guide pages alongside writing projects and other activities.

# STUDENT STUDY GUIDE: KEY FEATURES

The Student Study Guide works as both standalone instructional material and as a support to the Student Edition and this Teaching Guide. Certain activities encourage informal small-group or family participation. These features make it an effective teaching tool:

## Flexibility

You can use the Study Guide in the classroom, with individuals or small groups, or send it home for homework. You can distribute the entire guide to students; however, the pages are perforated so you can remove and distribute only the pertinent lessons.

A page on reports and special projects directs students to the "Further Reading" resource in the student edition. This feature gives students general guidance on doing research and devising independent study projects of their own.

### FACSIMILE SPREAD
The Study Guide begins with a facsimile spread from the Student Edition. This spread gives reading strategies and highlights key features: captions, primary sources, sidebars, headings, etymologies. The spread supplies the contextualization students need to fully understand the material.

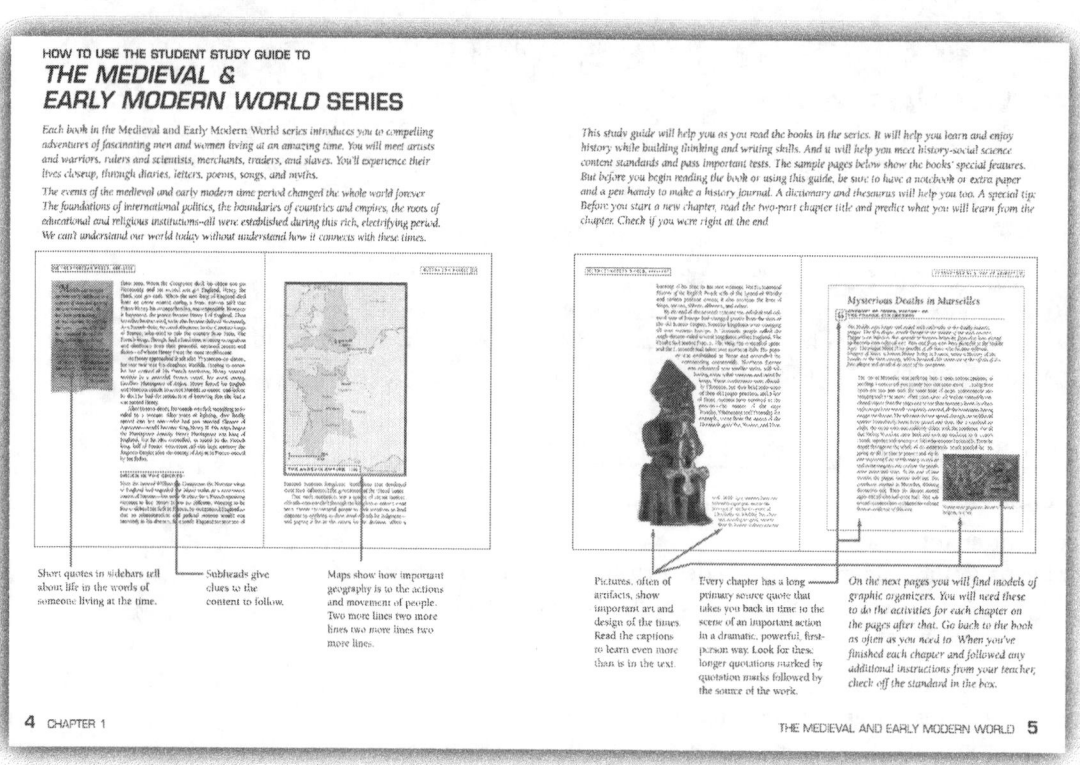

## Portfolio Approach

The Study Guide pages are three-hole-punched so they can be integrated with notebook paper in a looseleaf binder. This history journal or portfolio can become both a record of content mastery and an outlet for each student's unique creative expression. Responding to prompts, students can write poetry or songs, plays and character sketches, create storyboards or cartoons, or construct multi-layered timelines.

The portfolio approach gives students unlimited opportunities for practice in areas that need strengthening. Students can share their journals and compare their work. And the Study Guide pages in the portfolio make a valuable assessment tool for you. The portfolio is an ongoing record of performance that can be reviewed and graded periodically.

### GRAPHIC ORGANIZERS

This feature contains reduced models of seven graphic organizers referenced frequently in the study guide. Using these devices will help students organize the material so it is meaningful to them. (Full-size reproducibles of each graphic organizer are provided at the back of this Teaching Guide.) These graphic organizers include: outline, main idea map, K-W-L chart (What I Know, What I Want to Know, What I Learned), Venn diagram, timeline, sequence of events chart, and T-chart.

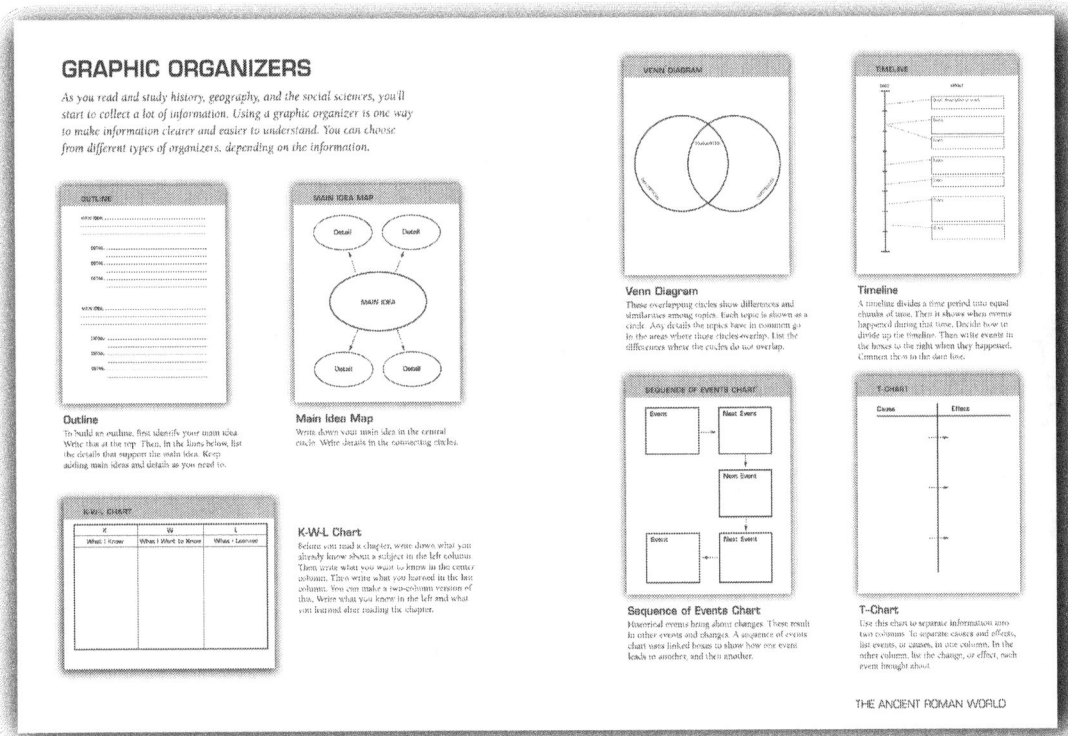

# STUDENT STUDY GUIDE: CHAPTER LESSONS

Each chapter lesson is designed to draw students into the subject matter. Recurring features and exercises challenge their knowledge and allow them to practice valuable analysis and English language arts skills. Activities in the Teaching Guide and Student Study Guide complement but do not duplicate each other. Together they offer a wide range of class work, group projects, and opportunities for further study and assessment that can be tailored to all ability levels.

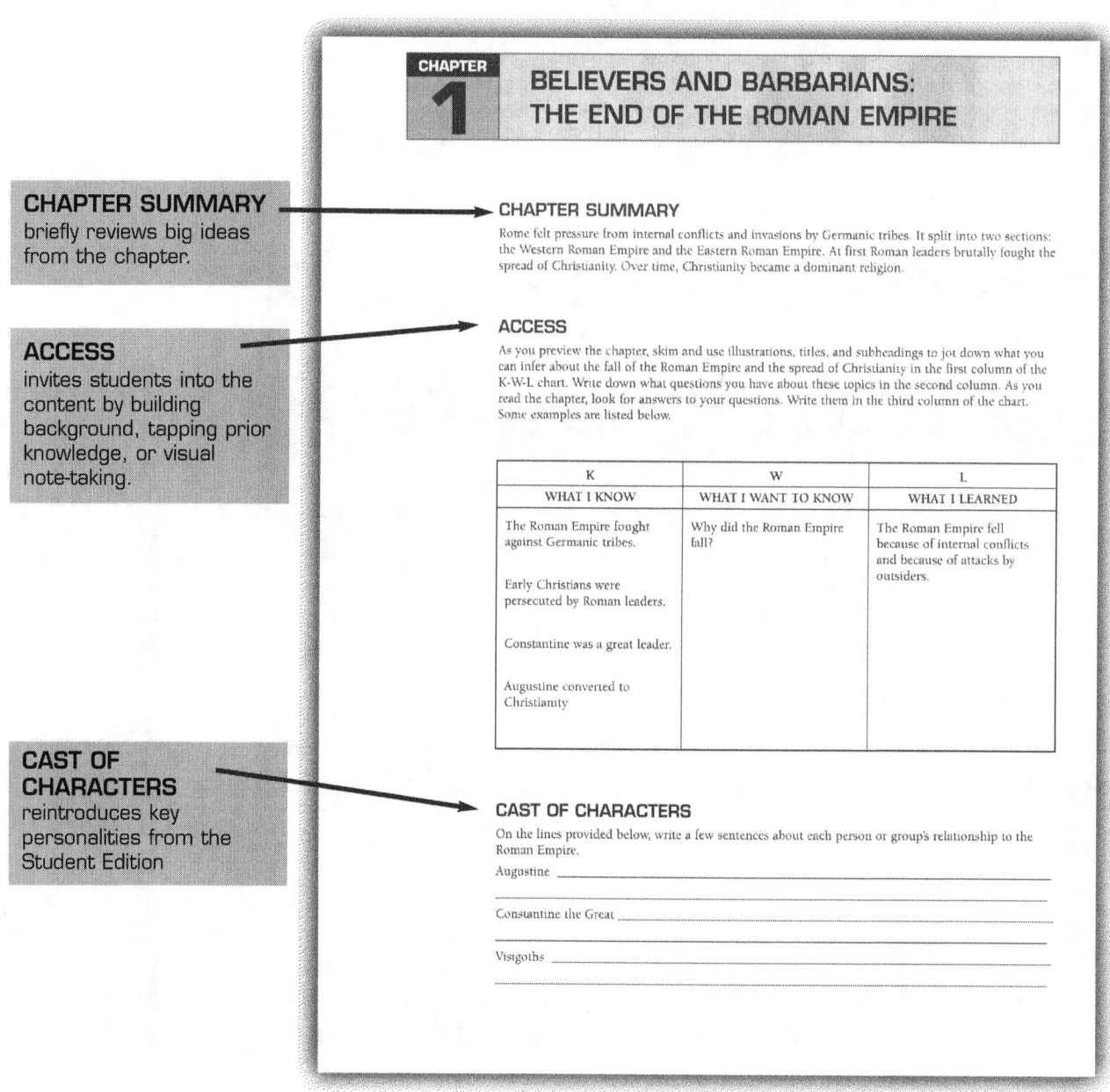

**CHAPTER SUMMARY** briefly reviews big ideas from the chapter.

**ACCESS** invites students into the content by building background, tapping prior knowledge, or visual note-taking.

**CAST OF CHARACTERS** reintroduces key personalities from the Student Edition

## CHAPTER 1: BELIEVERS AND BARBARIANS: THE END OF THE ROMAN EMPIRE

### CHAPTER SUMMARY
Rome felt pressure from internal conflicts and invasions by Germanic tribes. It split into two sections: the Western Roman Empire and the Eastern Roman Empire. At first Roman leaders brutally fought the spread of Christianity. Over time, Christianity became a dominant religion.

### ACCESS
As you preview the chapter, skim and use illustrations, titles, and subheadings to jot down what you can infer about the fall of the Roman Empire and the spread of Christianity in the first column of the K-W-L chart. Write down what questions you have about these topics in the second column. As you read the chapter, look for answers to your questions. Write them in the third column of the chart. Some examples are listed below.

| K<br>WHAT I KNOW | W<br>WHAT I WANT TO KNOW | L<br>WHAT I LEARNED |
|---|---|---|
| The Roman Empire fought against Germanic tribes.<br><br>Early Christians were persecuted by Roman leaders.<br><br>Constantine was a great leader.<br><br>Augustine converted to Christianity | Why did the Roman Empire fall? | The Roman Empire fell because of internal conflicts and because of attacks by outsiders. |

### CAST OF CHARACTERS
On the lines provided below, write a few sentences about each person or group's relationship to the Roman Empire.

Augustine _____

Constantine the Great _____

Visigoths _____

**WORD BANK** reintroduces key curricular terms and difficult words from the Student Edition.

**CRITICAL THINKING** exercises draw on such thinking skills as establishing cause and effect, making inferences, comparing and contrasting, identifying main ideas and details, and other analytical process.

**WORKING WITH PRIMARY SOURCES** invites students to read primary sources closely. Exercises include DBQ's, evaluating point of view, and writing.

**WRITE ABOUT IT** A writing assignment may stem from a vocabulary word, a historical event, or a primary source. The assignment can be a newspaper article, letter, short essay, a scene with dialogue, a diary entry.

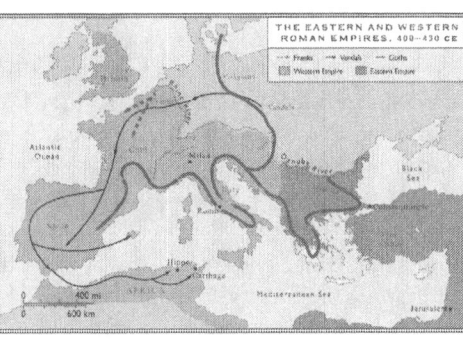

**ALL OVER THE MAP** uses engaging map skills activities to help students understand geography's crucial role in shaping history.

15

# IMPROVING LITERACY WITH THE MEDIEVAL & EARLY MODERN WORLD

The books in this series are written in a lively, narrative style to inspire a love of reading history. English language learners and struggling readers are given special consideration within the program's exercises and activities. And students who love to read and learn will also benefit from the program's rich and varied material. Following are strategies to make sure each and every student gets the most out of the subjects you will teach through *The Medieval & Early Modern World*.

## ENGLISH LANGUAGE LEARNERS

For English learners to achieve academic success, the instructional considerations for teachers include two mandates:

- Help them attain grade level, content area knowledge, and academic language.
- Provide for the development of English language proficiency.

To accomplish these goals, you should plan lessons that reflect the student's level of English proficiency. Students progress through five developmental levels as they increase in language proficiency:

> Beginning and Early Intermediate *(grade level material will be mostly incomprehensible, students need a great deal of teacher support)*
>
> Intermediate *(grade level work will be a challenge)*
>
> Early Advanced and Advanced *(close to grade level reading and writing, students continue to need support)*

Refer to your state's ELD Standards for information about language proficiency at each level. The books in this program are written at the intermediate level. However, you can still use the lesson plans for students of different levels by using the strategies below:

### Tap Prior Knowledge
What students know about the topic will help determine your next steps for instruction. Using K-W-L charts, brainstorming, and making lists are ways to find out what they know. English learners bring a rich cultural diversity into the classroom. By sharing what they know, students can connect their knowledge and experiences to the course.

### Set the Context
Use different tools to make new information understandable. These can be images, artifacts, maps, timelines, illustrations, charts, videos, or graphic organizers. Techniques such as role-playing and story-boarding can also be helpful. Speak in shorter sentences, with careful enunciation, expanded explanations, repetitions, and paraphrasing. Use fewer idiomatic expressions.

### Show—Don't Just Tell
English learners often get lost as they listen to directions, explanations, lectures, and discussions. By showing students what is expected, you can help them participate more fully in classroom activities. Students need to be shown how to use the graphic organizers in this guide and the mini versions in the student study guide, as well as other blackline masters for note-taking and practice. An overhead transparency with whole or small groups is also effective.

### Use the Text
Because of unfamiliar words, students will need help. Teach them to preview the chapter using text features (headings, bold print, sidebars, italics). See the suggestions in the facsimile of the Student Edition, shown on pages 6–7 of the Student Study Guide. Show students organizing structures such as cause and effect or comparing and contrasting. Have students read to each other in pairs. Encourage them to share their history journals with each other. Use Read Aloud/Think Aloud, perhaps with an overhead transparency. Help them create word banks, charts, and graphic organizers. Discuss the main idea after reading.

### Check for Understanding
Rather than simply ask students if they understand, stop frequently and ask them to paraphrase or expand on what you just said. Such techniques will give you a much clearer assessment of their understanding.

### Provide for Interaction
As students interact with the information and speak their thoughts, their content knowledge and academic language skills improve. Increase interaction in the classroom through cooperative learning, small group work, and partner share. By working and talking with others, students can practice asking and answering questions.

### Use Appropriate Assessment
When modifying the instruction, you will also need to modify the assessment. Multiple choice, true and false, and other criterion reference tests are suitable, but consider changing test format and structure. English learners are constantly improving their language proficiency in their oral and written responses, but they are often grammatically incorrect. Remember to be thoughtful and fair about giving students credit for their content knowledge and use of academic language, even if their English isn't perfect.

## STRUGGLING READERS

Some students struggle to understand the information presented in a textbook. The following strategies for content-area reading can help students improve their ability to make comparisons, sequence events, determine importance, summarize, evaluate, synthesize, analyze, and solve problems.

### Build Knowledge of Genre
Both the fiction and narrative nonfiction genres are incorporated into *The Medieval & Early Modern World*. This combination of genres makes the text interesting and engaging. But teachers must be sure students can identify and use the organizational structures of both genres.

| Fiction | Nonfiction |
| --- | --- |
| Each chapter is a story | Content: historical information |
| Setting: historical time and place | Organizational structure: cause/effect, sequence of events, problem/solution |
| Characters: historical figures | Other features: maps, timelines, sidebars, photographs, primary sources |
| Plot: problems, roadblocks, and resolutions | |

In addition, the textbook has a wealth of the text features of nonfiction: bold and italic print, sidebars, headings and subheadings, labels, captions, and "signal words" such as *first*, *next*, and *finally*. Teaching these organizational structures and text features is essential for struggling readers.

## Build Background

Having background information about a topic makes reading about it so much easier. When students lack background information, teachers can preteach or "front load" concepts and vocabulary, using a variety of instructional techniques. Conduct a chapter or book walk, looking at titles, headings, and other text features to develop a big picture of the content. Focus on new vocabulary words during the "walk" and create a word bank with illustrations for future reference. Read aloud key passages and discuss the meaning. Focus on the timeline and maps to help students develop a sense of time and place. Show a video, go to a website, and have trade books and magazines on the topic available for student exploration.

## Comprehension Strategies

While reading, successful readers are predicting, making connections, monitoring, visualizing, questioning, inferring, and summarizing. Struggling readers have a harder time with these "in the head" processes. The following strategies will help these students construct meaning from the text until they are able to do it on their own.

> **PREDICT:** Before reading, conduct a picture and text feature "tour" of the chapter to make predictions. Ask students if they remember if this has ever happened before, to predict what might happen this time.
>
> **MAKE CONNECTIONS:** Help students relate content to their background (text to text, text to self, and text to the world).
>
> **MONITOR AND CONFIRM:** Encourage students to stop reading when they come across an unknown word, phrase, or concept. In their notebooks, have them make a note of text they don't understand and ask for clarification or figure it out. While this activity slows down reading at first, it is effective in improving skills over time.
>
> **VISUALIZE:** Students benefit from imagining the events described in a story. Sketching scenes, story-boarding, role-playing, and looking for sensory details all help students with this strategy.
>
> **INFER:** Help students look beyond the literal meaning of a text to understand deeper meanings. Graphic organizers and discussions provide opportunities to broaden their understanding. Looking closely at the "why" of historical events helps students infer.
>
> **QUESTION AND DISCUSS:** Have students jot down their questions as they read, and then share them during discussions. Or have students come up with the type of questions they think a teacher would ask. Over time students will develop more complex inferential questions, which lead to group discussions. Questioning and discussing also helps students see ideas from multiple perspectives and draw conclusions, both critical skills for understanding history.

**DETERMINE IMPORTANCE:** Teach students how to decide what is most important from all the facts and details in nonfiction. After reading for an overall understanding, they can go back to highlight important ideas, words, and phrases. Clues for determining importance include bold or italic print, signal words, and other text features. A graphic organizer such as a main idea map also helps.

### Teach and Practice Decoding Strategies

Rather than simply defining an unfamiliar word, teach struggling readers decoding strategies:

- Have them look at the prefix, suffix, and root to help figure out the new word.
- Look for words they know within the word.
- Use the context for clues, and read further or reread.

## ADVANCED LEARNERS

Every classroom has students who finish the required assignments and then want additional challenges. Fortunately, the very nature of history and social science offers a wide range of opportunities for students to explore topics in greater depth. Encourage them to come up with their own ideas for an additional assignment. Determine the final product, its presentation, and a timeline for completion.

### ▶ Research

Students can develop in-depth understanding through seeking information, exploring ideas, asking and answering questions, making judgments, considering points of view, and evaluating actions and events. They will need access to a wide range of resource materials: the Internet, maps, encyclopedias, trade books, magazines, dictionaries, artifacts, newspapers, museum catalogues, brochures, and the library. See the "Further Reading" section at the end of the Student Edition for good jumping-off points.

### ▶ Projects

You can encourage students to capitalize on their strengths as learners (visual, verbal, kinesthetic, or musical) or to try a new way of responding. Students can prepare a debate or write a persuasive paper, play, skit, poem, song, dance, game, puzzle, or biography. They can create an alphabet book on the topic, film a video, do a book talk, or illustrate a book. They can render charts, graphs, or other visual representations. Allow for creativity and support students' thinking.

Cheryl A. Caldera, M.A.
Literacy Coach

# GROUP PROJECTS

These interactive, multimedia projects give every student the chance to experience some aspect of life in *An Age of Voyages, 1350–1600*. They will add fun and depth to your exploration of this amazing time in history and can be used for assessment with the rubrics at the back of this Teaching Guide.

## Chapter 1
### ▶ Research Report

Invite students to work in small groups to frame questions about and then research topics discussed in Chapter 1. Possible topics include the Hundred Years' War, plague and other epidemics, Giovanni Boccaccio, the importance of the Silk Road and other trade routes during Mongol rule, and Zhu Yuanzhang.

In addition to having each group prepare a written report, invite each group to share its findings with the rest of the class by preparing an oral report accompanied by a visual display. Remind presenters to use effective speaking techniques, including enunciation and eye contact, when sharing their reports.

As an additional assessment for this research report, use the Group Project rubric at the back of this guide. Have students rate their own work with the self-assessment rubric.

## Chapter 2
### ▶ Live Renaissance Exhibition

Create a living history exhibition about the Renaissance for a school or community audience. Have students choose their roles. Some students may portray figures from the Cast of Characters; others may take on the roles of people from different social classes and occupations. Some may choose to depict "living" representations of Renaissance paintings. Suggest that a few students play harlequins, who will guide the audience through the exhibition. Tell each student to research his or her role and prepare a speech to explain his or her part.

As an additional assessment for the Renaissance Exhibition, have students portraying related characters work together to gauge their understanding of the era. Use the Group Project rubric at the back of this guide to assess students' work, and have students rate their own work with the self-assessment rubric.

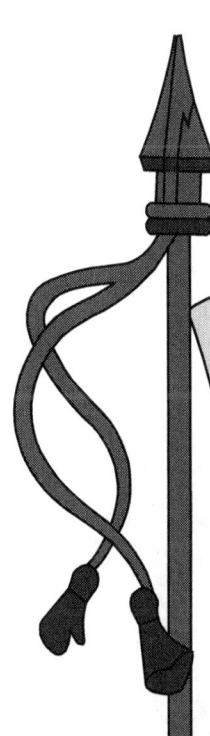

## Chapter 3
### ▸ Investigate the Great Wall of China

Interested students can frame questions about the Great Wall that can be answered by historical research. For example, they might investigate why the wall was not helpful in resisting large invasions, what life was like for the hundreds of thousands of people who worked on it, or what the Great Wall is like today. Suggest that they work with partners to make a scale model or diagram of a section of the Great Wall and orally describe its features and the materials used to make it.

As an additional assessment of partners' understanding of the history and function of the Great Wall, use the Group Project rubric at the back of this guide. Have partners rate their own work with the self-assessment rubric.

## Chapter 4
### ▸ Research Report

Have students work together in small groups to research and prepare reports on such topics as:

- The Life and Accomplishments of Johan Gutenberg
- Early Woodblock Printing in China and Korea
- The Production of Parchment, Vellum, and Early Paper
- Printers Unite! The Formation of Craft Guilds

Tell students to frame questions to focus the research. Direct groups to assign specific tasks to each member, and to work together to complete their report. Encourage them to include illustrations, maps, charts, and other graphic aids. Provide classroom time for oral presentations, followed by bulletin board display.

As an additional assessment for this research report, use the Group Project rubric at the back of this guide. Have students rate their own work with the self-assessment rubric.

## Chapter 5
### ▸ Timeline of Pacifism

As pacifist Protestant groups such as the Quakers moved to other parts of the world, they spread their beliefs. Have small groups research the history of pacifism through the centuries. Suggest they create a timeline in which they identify key pacifists, such as Cesar Chavez and Dr. Martin Luther King, Jr., and elaborate on their lives and actions. Encourage students to expand their timelines with quotes from speeches, letters, and diaries.

As an additional assessment of students' understanding of the history of pacifism, use the Group Project rubric at the back of this guide. Have students rate their own work with the self-assessment rubric.

## Chapter 6
### ▸ Chronology

Students can create parallel timelines showing chapter events that happened in Europe and Asia. For example, two timelines might include events that trace the growth of the Ottoman and Mughal Empires. Another timeline might include events in Europe, especially the rise of Ferdinand and Isabella, and the Spanish Inquisition. Another timeline might describe the spread and decline of Muslim rule in Europe and Asia.

Assess students' awareness of the chronology of events in the various empires by having them work in small groups to analyze and compare their timelines. Use the Group Project rubric at the back of this guide to assess students' work, and have students rate their own work with the self-assessment rubric.

## Chapter 7
### ▶ The Plot Thickens

As noted in the Student Edition, the early life of Elizabeth Tudor sounds like the plot of a soap opera. Have groups of students use the information provided in the text to create storyboards for the events leading up to Elizabeth's reign. Some group members can review the text to match the events described on pages 99–100 to the names and titles provided on page 101. Others can plan a logical sequence of events for the storyboards and create the displays. Allow time for groups to present their storyboards.

## Chapter 8
### ▶ Travel Brochure

Invite students to work in small groups to create a travel brochure for one of the cities that they read about in Chapter 8. Explain that the travel brochure should reflect what the city was like in the late 1400s to mid-1600s. Direct students to research the city's history, architecture, arts, religious sites, and economy. They might also note the city's class structure, occupations, customs, foods, and holidays. Encourage students to create visuals and, if possible, a map of the city. Explain that the travel brochures should be designed to appeal to travelers, so students should take care to use persuasive language and appealing images. Suggest that students create catchy headings for each section of their brochure, such as *Cultural Do's and Don'ts*. Remind students to proofread and edit their brochures before finalizing them. Allow time for each group to present their completed brochures to their classmates and to summarize orally the attractions of the city they researched. Follow each presentation with a question-and-answer period.

Assess each group's understanding of medieval city life using the Group Project rubric at the back of this guide. Have students rate their own work with the self-assessment rubric.

### Chapter 9
▶ **Silk Showcase**

Have students work in small groups to investigate the making and uses of silk in the 15th century. Brainstorm a variety of related topics, such as how and where silk was made, trade routes along which silk was sold, and silk clothing in 15th century art works. Invite each group to frame questions related to their topic and to conduct the research to find answers.

Direct groups to assign specific tasks to each member, and to work together to prepare an oral presentation. Encourage them to include visuals, such as diagrams, illustrations, maps, charts, and other graphic aids in their presentations. Provide classroom time for presentations, and have groups display the visuals they use in a Silk Showcase.

Use the Group Project rubric at the back of this guide to assess students' understanding of the impact of silk trade on the medieval world. Have students rate their own work with the self-assessment rubric.

### Chapter 10
▶ **Caravels, Inside and Out**

Invite pairs of students to conduct research to learn more about why caravels, like the ones Columbus sailed, were well suited to cross the Atlantic Ocean. Suggest that they make a scale model or a diagram of a caravel to include with oral presentations. Students may find useful information to begin their research at *www.bestscalemodels.com/santamaria.html*.

To assess partners' understanding of the design of caravels, use the Group Project rubric at the back of this guide. Have students rate their own work with the self-assessment rubric.

## Chapter 11
▶ **Plantation Images**

Create a classroom library of images related to sugar plantations and slavery. Have pairs of students work together to use electronic and print resources to research and collect artworks and illustrations that tell about life on sugar plantations and slavery. Tell students to make note of artists, locations, and subjects when appropriate. Invite students to write captions about the images as they add them to the library. Consider asking pairs to select some of their work for binding into a class book.

Use the Group Project rubric at the back of this guide to assess partners' understanding of life on a sugar plantation. Have students rate their own work with the self-assessment rubric.

## Chapter 12
▶ **Chronology**

Help students identify connections between events in Central and South America that were relatively close in time. For example, the Spanish invasion of the capitals of the Aztec and Inca empires occurred 14 years apart. Ask students to recall what they learned in earlier chapters to infer how the two events were related. What technology enabled the Spanish to cross the Atlantic? What weapons allowed them to defeat the Aztecs and the Incas? Why did Christianity spread to both regions? How did events on Caribbean sugar plantations lead to the conquests of the Aztecs and Incas? Small groups can create charts and timelines showing the related events and the conclusions they draw about their causes.

To assess each small group's grasp of the interconnected events in Central and South America, use the Group Project rubric at the back of this guide. Have students rate their own work with the self-assessment rubric.

# CHAPTER 1

# DISEASE AND DISASTER: THE DREADFUL 14TH CENTURY
## PAGES 14–25

**FOR HOMEWORK**

Student Study Guide pages 11–14

## CHAPTER SUMMARY

Disasters such as war and plague occurred in many parts of the world in the 14th century, causing many changes. As plague spread along trade routes and with Mongol armies from China, it killed millions. The epidemic added to the misery of war and left fewer peasants and workers to labor. Yet in the long run, life improved for many plague survivors. In China, Zhu Yuanzhang led rebels to capture the Mongol capital Khanbalik and founded the Ming dynasty.

## PERFORMANCE OBJECTIVES

- To understand the causes and effects of plague and war in the 1300s
- To understand the importance of trade routes in spreading the plague
- To describe the spread of bubonic plague from China to the Middle East, Northern Africa, and Europe

## BUILDING BACKGROUND

Discuss some common illnesses, such as colds and the flu, or childhood diseases, such as chicken pox or measles. Elicit that people who come in close contact with such illnesses often become sick themselves and explain that plague and other epidemics spread in similar ways. Ask students to speculate about the effects of epidemics and to identify ways that people deal with epidemics.

## VOCABULARY

**contagious** easily spread

**famine** a shortage of food

**peasants** members of a low-ranking social class, often farmers and laborers

**landlords** landowners who lease or rent their land to others

**nobles** members of a high-ranking class who are often wealthy and powerful

**caravans** a group of travelers journeying together for safety

As needed, have students consult the glossary to define the following words: *buboes, dynasty, flagellants.*

## WORKING WITH PRIMARY SOURCES

Direct attention to the quotations from John VI on Student Edition page 17. Ask students to identify words and phrases he uses to indicate the power of the disease. Discuss why an emperor would be unaccustomed to the lack of control that resulted from the epidemic.

**CAST OF CHARACTERS**

**Petrarch** (PEE-trahrk), **Francesco** (fran-CHESS-koh) Italian scholar, humanist, and poet

**Hongwu** founder of the Ming dynasty in China, began life as **Zhu** (ju) **Yuanzhang** (yun-JANG)

**Boccaccio** (boh-KAH-chee-oh), **Giovanni** (joh-VAHN-nee) Italian writer, best known for the *Decameron* (deh-KAMM-ehr-on)

26  CHAPTER 1

## GEOGRAPHY CONNECTION

**Movement** Direct attention to the map on Student Edition page 15. Help students use the map key to identify the areas where the first outbreaks of the plague occurred. Explain that the arrows show the direction in which the plague spread from those areas. Ask students to use their fingers to trace the routes of the plague's spread and to identify the regions and cities affected by the plague.

## READING COMPREHENSION QUESTIONS

1. What two things made the 14th century terrible in Europe, Asia, and North Africa? (*plague and wars*)
2. What effects did the Hundred Years' War have on France? (*The French countryside was devastated, crops were stolen, villages were burned, animals and people were killed, and taxes were increased to pay for the war.*)
3. How did plague spread from rats to humans? (*Fleas living on rats infected with the plague bacteria drink their blood. The bacteria that cause plague multiply in the flea's gut, and the flea passes the disease on to the next creature it bites. If a flea jumps from a rat to a human, the human can get the disease.*)
4. What did 14th-century people think caused bubonic plague? (*The following were considered causes of plague: poisoned or "corrupted" air, God, and the poisoning of wells by Jews. Chinese doctors thought the life force of the body could not flow freely, which caused an imbalance between the yin and yang.*)
5. How did the plague spread from China to other parts of Asia, North Africa, and Europe? (*Plague-infested rats accompanied Mongol armies and also merchants who traveled along trade routes from China to other parts of the world.*)

## CRITICAL THINKING QUESTIONS

1. Why were doctors in the 14th century unable to keep the plague from killing millions of people? (*They didn't know what caused the plague, nor did they know how to prevent it or cure it.*)
2. Where would the plague have spread if southwestern China had been isolated from the rest of the world in the 14th century? (*The plague would probably have been contained in southwestern China and wouldn't have spread elsewhere.*)
3. Over the long run, why do you think there was improvement in the social and economic lives of those peasants and workers who survived plague? (*Possible answer: There were fewer people to do the work that landlords and employers needed to have done. Therefore peasants and workers were in a better position to bargain with their employers and to have their demands met.*)

## SOCIAL SCIENCES

**Science, Technology, and Society** Remind students that Chinese doctors thought about the body in terms of flow and balance and used acupuncture and medicines to treat illnesses. Invite groups of students to investigate Chinese methods of treatment and to prepare oral reports to share their findings.

---

### THEN and NOW

Millions of people died from plague in the Middle Ages. Today antibiotics can often cure some illnesses if an infected person is treated promptly, and vaccinations prevent many diseases that once resulted in epidemics. New diseases like HIV/AIDS can still be very deadly, however. HIV/AIDS is now the fourth-leading cause of death in the world.

### LINKING DISCIPLINES

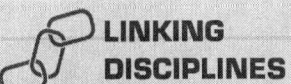

**Health** Have students research how people today prevent and cure epidemic illnesses such as the plague. Ask how people in the 14th century could have used resources that were available then to prevent plague, if only they had known how it spread.

---

AN AGE OF VOYAGES, 1350–1600

## LITERATURE CONNECTION

There are numerous enjoyable books that will broaden students' knowledge of life in the time of the plague.

Cantor, Norman. *In the Wake of the Plague: The Black Death and the World It Made.* New York: Perennial, 2002. Nonfiction. The author details the causes and devastating effects of plague in Europe. **ADVANCED**

DeAngeli, Marguerite. *The Door in the Wall.* New York: Yearling, 1990. Historical Fiction. In this award-winning story, a 14th-century boy becomes a hero as the plague devastates London. **EASY**

Ellis, Deborah. *A Company of Fools.* Markham, Ontario: Fitzhenry & Whiteside Limited, 2002. Historical Fiction. Two choir boys from a Parisian abbey sing to cheer the city's population as plague changes the life they once knew. **EASY**

## LITERACY TIPS

In addition to using the suggestions in the Supporting Learning and Extending Learning sections, refer back frequently to pages 16–19 for strategies and advice from a literacy coach.

## READING AND LANGUAGE ARTS

**Reading Nonfiction** Direct students to complete a sequence of events chart (at the back of the book) to show the start of the plague, how it spread, and its effects on people. Tell students to use the chart to help them summarize the events described in the chapter. Use this activity to assess students' understanding of the main ideas of the chapter.

**Using Language** Have students list the descriptive language and exact words the author uses to describe the plague. Then have students use words from their list to write their own description of the plague.

## WRITING

**News Article** Invite students to imagine they are reporters assigned to describe what is happening in a plague-infested European city in 1348. Direct students to write *who, what, when, where, why,* and *how* questions and answer them in their articles.

## SUPPORTING LEARNING

**English Language Learners** Guide students to identify and categorize words related to the plague as they read the chapter. Suggest that they list and define words in their history journals as they read. Students might categorize words that are synonymous with illness (*disease, plague, infection*), words that describe symptoms (*headache, nausea, feverish, buboes, swelling*), or words that suggest the plague's possible causes (*contagious, poison, germs*).

**Struggling Readers** Read aloud the first paragraph on Student Edition page 14. Model how to analyze text to determine causes and effects. Read aloud the second paragraph on pages 15–16 and ask questions to guide students in identifying causes and effects, such as: *What caused the fighting between England and France?* Have students read the rest of the chapter with a partner, stopping after each paragraph to list causes and effects in a chart. You may wish to have students use the cause and effect graphic organizer at the back of this guide to record the information.

## EXTENDING LEARNING

**Enrichment** Invite students to use Internet and nonfiction library resources to investigate trade routes, such as the Silk Road, that connected China with other parts of the world during the Middle Ages. Students may create maps and visuals to use during an oral presentation to share their findings.

**Extension** Have students work in groups to write a skit in which 14th-century villagers try to persuade one another about the best way to combat and prevent the plague. Allow time for groups to rehearse and perform their skits.

NAME _____ DATE _____

**An Age of Voyages, 1350–1600**

## SPREAD OF THE BLACK DEATH, 1333–1369

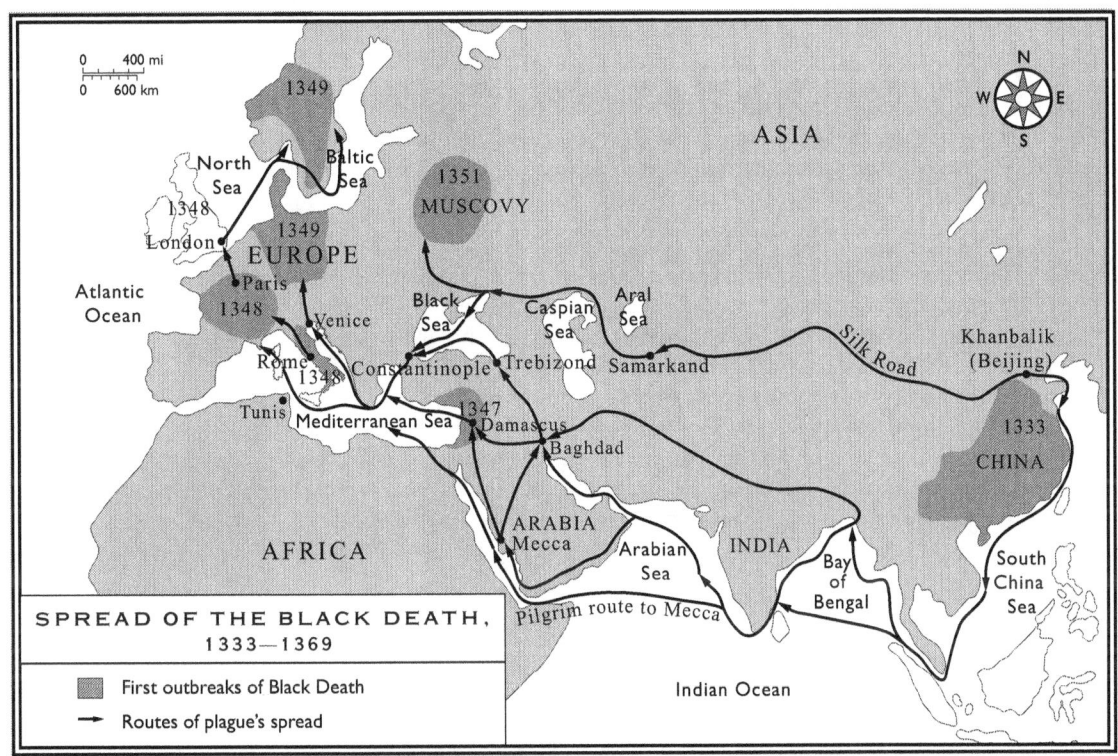

**Directions**

Use the map to answer the questions that follow.

1. Describe the path of the Black Death as it spread from the area around Khanbalik to other parts of the world.
   _____

2. Use the scale of miles to calculate the approximate distance that the plague spread between Khanbalik and Samarkand.
   _____

3. When did the Black Death reach Damascus?
   _____

4. What routes did the plague spread along to reach Baghdad?
   _____
   _____

5. How many years did it take for the plague to spread from Khanbalik to London?
   _____
   _____

CHAPTER 1 BLM  AN AGE OF VOYAGES, 1350–1600  **29**

**NAME**             **DATE**

## GOOD HOUSEKEEPING IN 1393

**Directions**

The following text is from *The Medieval & Early Modern World Primary Sources and Reference Volume*, pages 34–35. In it, a middle-class citizen advises his much younger wife how to run the household well and how to treat him to ensure his happiness. Read the advice with a partner, and answer the questions that follow. If necessary, use a dictionary for help with the meanings of unfamiliar words.

> And in summer take heed that there be no fleas in your chamber, nor in your bed. . . . I have heard from several that if the room be strewn with alder leaves, the fleas will be caught thereon. Item I have heard tell that if you have at night one or two trenchers [of bread] slimed with glue or turpentine and set about the room, with a lighted candle in the midst of each trencher, they will come and be stuck thereto. The other way that I have tried and 'tis true: take a rough cloth and spread it about your room and over your bed, and all the fleas that shall hop thereon will be caught, so that you may carry them away with the cloth. . . . I have seen blanchets [of white wool] set upon the straw and on the bed, and when the black fleas hopped thereon, they were the sooner found upon the white, and killed.

1. Think about what you have learned about the plague. Why does this text do a good job of illustrating conditions that helped plague to spread?

2. What was probably a common summertime problem in the 1300s? How can you tell?

3. Which method of catching fleas do you think would be the most successful? Why?

4. Why do you think this advice was written?

NAME _____ DATE _____

## A. MULTIPLE CHOICE

**Circle the letter of the best answer for each question.**

1. Which of the following was **not** an effect of the Hundred Years' War?
   a. The French countryside was devastated.
   b. Plague broke out.
   c. Villages were burned.
   d. People and animals died.

2. Which of the following describes why Chinese peasants revolted in the late 1300s?
   a. Landlords raised taxes.
   b. Plague broke out.
   c. Mongol rulers encouraged foreign trade.
   d. Peasants had to work longer and harder.

3. Why did people get sick and die from plague?
   a. They had no resistance to plague.
   b. Taxes were too high.
   c. The air was poisoned.
   d. People had sinned.

4. What happened as a result of rumors that Jews were spreading plague by poisoning wells?
   a. People stopped drinking water.
   b. Flagellants whipped themselves.
   c. Christians tortured and killed Jews.
   d. Christians went on pilgrimages.

## B. CAUSE AND EFFECT

**Complete the chart by writing a cause for each effect.**

| CAUSE | EFFECT |
|---|---|
| 5. | The people of Kaffa became infected with plague. |
| 6. | People held strong-smelling herbs, such as rosemary, in front of their noses. |
| 7. | Peasants got more food, better clothing, and slightly larger farms. |

## C. MAP

**Use the map on Student Edition page 15 to answer the question.**

4. Use your finger to trace one of the routes of the plague's spread from Baghdad to Venice. Write a paragraph to describe that route here.

_____
_____
_____

AN AGE OF VOYAGES, 1350–1600                              CHAPTER 1 TEST   **31**

# CHAPTER 2: RENAISSANCE MEN AND RENAISSANCE MONEY: LEARNING AND ART IN ITALY AND BEYOND    PAGES 26–4[]

**Student Study Guide pages 15–18**

### CAST OF CHARACTERS

**Leonardo** (lee-uh-NAHR-doh) **da Vinci** (duh VIHN-chee) Italian Renaissance artist, engineer, and inventor

**Medici** (MEHD-ih-chee) **Lorenzo de'** (law-REN-dzow day) ruler of Florence

**Michelangelo** (MY-kuhl-AN-juh-loh) **Buonarotti** (bwah-nah-RAH-tee) Italian Renaissance artist, poet, and architect

**Machiavelli**, (MAH-kee-uf-VEHL-lee), **Niccolò** (nee-coh-LOW) government official and writer from Florence, author of *The Prince*

**Cervantes** (sehr-VAHN-tehs), **Miguel de** (mee-GEHL deh) Spanish author and playwright whose best-known work is *Don Quixote*

**Shakespeare, William** English playwright and poet

## CHAPTER SUMMARY

The era known as the Renaissance began during the 15th century as a revival of classical thinking and arts. Centered in Italian cities, the era ushered in a time of remarkable advances in education and the arts and sciences; the works of numerous important thinkers from this time form the basis of western traditions still followed and studied today.

## PERFORMANCE OBJECTIVES

▶ To trace the rise of Italian cities as centers of trade and learning during the Renaissance

▶ To describe how the revival of classical learning and arts led to the development of the concept of humanism

▶ To analyze advances in the arts and sciences during the Renaissance

▶ To identify the contributions made by figures such as da Vinci, Lorenzo de' Medici, Petrarch, Michelangelo, Machiavelli, Cervantes, and Shakespeare

## BUILDING BACKGROUND

Ask students to identify someone they know who is good at many things, and make a list of their responses. Tell students that they will learn about the time known as the Renaissance in this chapter. As they read, ask students to look for examples that help explain why the concept of multiple talents became associated with this era.

## VOCABULARY

**profit** the money that remains after a business pays its expenses

**theory** ideas and observations that have not been scientifically proven

**diplomat** a person who represents a government in its relations with others

**self-portrait** pictures of people created by themselves

**three dimensions** height, width, and depth in the visual arts

**material world** the physical world, as separate from the intellectual or spiritual

**moral code** one's system of distinguishing good from evil

**romantic** relating to fictional, heroic adventures

As needed, have students consult the glossary to define the following words: *apprentice, humanism, Renaissance, virtù*.

## WORKING WITH PRIMARY SOURCES

Point out Leonardo's *Mona Lisa* on Student Edition page 26. Explain that the subject is believed to be the wife of Francesco del Giocondo, which explains the painting's alternative title, "La Gioconda." Have students research the famous painting to learn more about its subject.

## GEOGRAPHY CONNECTION

**Region** Have students compare the map on page 29 to a current map of the region. Discuss territorial borders in 1450 and compare them to present-day national borders.

## READING COMPREHENSION QUESTIONS

1. How did Italian cities come to be ruled by the families of merchants, such as the Medici family in Florence? (*Over time, merchants like the Medicis freed their cities from the control of nobles and ruled through city councils.*)

2. What was the new type of education known as humanism? (*Humanism returned to the classical ideas of the Greeks and Romans and valued intellectual ideas and individual achievements.*)

3. What did Machiavelli's concept of *virtù* mean? (*Machiavelli believed that effective rulers were different from private people and possessed* virtù, *an ability to shape the world.*)

4. Why was Leonardo da Vinci seen as a genius? (*He was not only a brilliant artist; he was also an inventor and a scientist.*)

5. How did the Renaissance give rise to new literary languages? (*Prior to the Renaissance, Latin was the language used in writing. During the Renaissance, writers began to write in languages such as Italian, French, and Spanish that previously had been only spoken languages.*)

## CRITICAL THINKING QUESTIONS

1. Do you think that the arts and sciences could have blossomed during the Renaissance without the support of people like Lorenzo de' Medici? (*The money that supported arts and sciences was key during the Renaissance; funding from people such as de' Medici made it possible for talented people to live comfortably as they worked and studied.*)

2. Why do you think Renaissance artists strived for realism and emotion in their works? (*Creating realistic representations and showing emotion showed the importance of the mind and humanistic ideals.*)

3. How do the plays of Shakespeare reflect the power of humanist ideas? (*Some of his plays are directly or indirectly related to Greek and Roman history; they all center on human concerns and behavior.*)

## SOCIAL SCIENCES

**Science, Technology, and Society** Leonardo da Vinci's notebooks are filled with ideas for mechanical inventions that were ahead of their time. His studies of the human body's appearance and function are considered to be the first accurate drawings of the human anatomy. Invite students to research Leonardo's methods of study and prepare oral reports to share their findings.

---

### THEN and NOW

It took Michelangelo about five years to paint the ceiling of the Sistine Chapel. Over the centuries, pollution and other environmental factors darkened the works considerably. From 1979 to 1994, the images were cleaned and restored to their original condition, and a special air-filtering system was installed. To see a before-and-after comparison of cleaned images, go to http://sun.science.wayne.edu/~mcogan/humanities/sistine/ceiling/comparison.html.

###  LINKING DISCIPLINES

**Art** Use the paintings included in the chapter and others of your own choosing to lead a discussion on how Renaissance artists used elements such as perspective, composition, and light and shadow to help the viewer "see" their ideas.

---

AN AGE OF VOYAGES, 1350–1600

## LITERATURE CONNECTION

There are numerous enjoyable books that will broaden students' knowledge of the Renaissance.

Blackwood, Gary. *The Shakespeare Stealer*. London: Puffin Books, 2000. Historical Fiction. A rival theater manager sends a 14-year-old boy to the Globe Theater with orders to steal Shakespeare's *Hamlet*, or face the consequences.
AVERAGE

Konigsburg, E.L. *The Second Mrs. Gioconda*. New York: Aladdin, 1998. Historical Fiction. An apprentice for Leonardo da Vinci shares the story behind the painting of the Mona Lisa.
AVERAGE

McLanathan, Richard. *First Impressions: Michelangelo*. New York: Harry N. Abrams, 1993. Nonfiction. This book examines the achievements of the artist Michelangelo in the political world of Renaissance Italy.
ADVANCED

## LITERACY TIPS

In addition to using the suggestions in the Supporting Learning and Extending Learning sections, refer back frequently to pages 16–19 for strategies and advice from a literacy coach.

## READING AND LANGUAGE ARTS

**Reading Nonfiction** Point out that using text features can help students preview, understand, and review the information in the chapter. Ask students to identify text features such as titles, subtitles, section headings, images, and captions, and guide them to use these features to help them organize what they are learning.

**Using Language** Review the quotations from Cervantes' writing on Student Edition pages 37–38 and have students identify and analyze the metaphors he uses. Discuss how his choice of words allows the audience to think about things in a new way. Use the activity to assess students' understanding of the new ways of thinking that began during the Renaissance.

## WRITING

**Persuasive Essay** Have students take on the role of Francesco Petrarch and write a short persuasive essay to convince others of his time about the importance of Greek and Roman history and the ideas of humanism.

## SUPPORTING LEARNING

**English Language Learners** Use the central idea of rebirth during the Renaissance to discuss contrasts in ways of thinking and in language. For beginning learners, have students practice using sets of antonyms such as *rich/poor*, *light/dark*, and *moral/immoral*. Have small groups of intermediate and advanced learners locate antonyms used in the chapter and discuss how ideas during the Renaissance contrasted with those of the preceding period, which Renaissance thinkers called "dark."

**Struggling Readers** Guide students to create a web that describes Leonardo da Vinci and his accomplishments. Then have students create similar webs for others from the Cast of Characters. Invite students to compare and discuss their webs.

## EXTENDING LEARNING

**Enrichment** Though St. Benedict intended Monte Cassino to be a place of peace and refuge, its history is marked by upheaval and destruction. Ask students to research the monastery to learn more about its past. They may also learn about its current state at *www.officine.it/montecassino/main_e.htm*. Suggest that students create an illustrated and annotated timeline in their history journals to show the key events in Monte Cassino's history.

**Extension** The visual artists of the Renaissance were the first to create self-portraits. As a class, discuss why this idea may have developed and what information self-portraits provide. Invite students to create their own self-portraits, and create a gallery for students to present and discuss their work.

NAME _____ DATE _____

## EUROPE IN 1450

**Directions**

Use the map to answer the questions that follow.

1. Which central European territory was the largest in area?
   _____

2. Who ruled central Italy in 1450? What was his territory called?
   _____
   _____

3. What made Italy a good location for trading and exchanging ideas?
   _____
   _____

4. Why do you think wealthy merchants sought to control Italian cities?
   _____
   _____

5. Use the scale of miles to tell how far humanist ideas "traveled" from Florence to London.
   _____
   _____

CHAPTER 2 BLM        AN AGE OF VOYAGES, 1350–1600        **35**

**CHAPTER 2 BLM** — AN AGE OF VOYAGES, 1350–1600

NAME _____ DATE _____

## THE WONDROUS WORKS OF NATURE

**Directions**

This excerpt from Leonardo da Vinci's notebooks also appears on Student Edition page 33. Read the excerpt with a partner, and answer the questions that follow.

> The mind of the painter must resemble a mirror, which always takes the color of the object it reflects.... Therefore you must know, O painter! That you cannot be a good one if you are not the universal master of representing by your art every kind of form produced by nature.... The eye, which is called the window of the soul, is the principal means by which the central sense can most completely and abundantly appreciate the infinite works of nature; and the ear is the second, which acquires dignity by hearing of the things the eye has seen. If you, historians or poets or mathematicians, had not seen things with your eyes you could not report of them in writing.... We, by our arts, may be called the grandsons of God.
>
> And you, O Man, who will discern in this work of mine the wondrous works of nature, if you think it would be a criminal thing to destroy it, reflect how much more criminal it is to take the life of a man, and if this, his external form, appears to you marvelously constructed, remember that it is nothing as compared with the soul that dwells in that structure; for that indeed is a thing divine.

**1.** What types of readers does Leonardo address in this excerpt?

_____
_____
_____
_____

**2.** How does Leonardo support his idea that the eye is, as he calls it, "the central sense"?

_____
_____
_____
_____

**3.** What do you think Leonardo means when he says that artists are "the grandsons of God"?

_____
_____
_____
_____

**4.** How does Leonardo compare the human body to the human soul?

_____
_____
_____
_____

# CHAPTER TEST 2
### An Age of Voyages, 1350–1600

NAME _____ DATE _____

## A. MULTIPLE CHOICE

**Circle the letter of the best answer for each question.**

1. The ideas of humanism during the Renaissance developed from
   a. the works of ancient Greek and Roman writers, thinkers, and artists.
   b. scientific discoveries and the importance of laboratory experiments.
   c. a new interest in how the human body worked.
   d. the writings of Niccolò Machiavelli about how rulers should treat their subjects.

2. Humanists especially valued
   a. scientific ideas over religious ideas.
   b. effective but fair rulers.
   c. talented individuals who achieved beyond their backgrounds.
   d. artworks that depicted the importance of wealth.

3. Which of the following was not part of monastic life?
   a. copying manuscripts
   b. educating children
   c. governing towns
   d. praying

4. Some of Michelangelo's greatest works
   a. are portraits of the patrons who supported him in his work.
   b. were inventions that were ahead of their time.
   c. are the paintings and frescoes that adorn the Sistine Chapel.
   d. can be traced to his remarkable studies of human anatomy.

5. The plays of William Shakespeare have had a lasting appeal because
   a. of the debate about whether the plays were indeed written by him.
   b. they portray all kinds of people with universal human ideas and behavior.
   c. they require an educated audience to understand their ideas.
   d. almost all of them tell of well-known historical figures.

## B. MAIN IDEA/DETAILS

**Complete the chart by adding details that tell about the main idea.**

| MAIN IDEA | DETAILS |
|---|---|
| Italian cities such as Florence and Venice were key in spreading ideas of the Renaissance. | 1. _____ <br> 2. _____ <br> 3. _____ |

## C. ESSAY

Renaissance artists were the first to paint self-portraits and to sign their works of art. On a separate sheet of paper, write an essay to explain how these actions reflect the ideals of humanism.

# CHAPTER 3

# GHOSTS, MONKEYS, OR CONFUCIUS: LEARNING AS POWER IN MING CHINA PAGES 41–53

**FOR HOMEWORK**

Student Study Guide pages 19–22

**CAST OF CHARACTERS**

**Tang** (tahng) **Xianzu** (shyen-ZOO) Chinese playwright, author of *The Peony Pavilion*

**Wang** (wong) **Yangming** (yahng-MING) neo-Confucian scholar

**Yongle** (yong-leh) Ming emperor, sent naval expeditions to Indian Ocean

## CHAPTER SUMMARY

In 1368, Zhu Yuanzhang defeated the Mongols and declared himself the emperor of northern China. He renamed himself Hongwu and named his dynasty Ming, or "brilliant." He promoted Confucius's belief in obedience to authority. Government jobs went to nobles and commoners who passed rigorous exams. The Ming emperors extended the Great Wall and oversaw a growing economy and population. Foreign trade brought new markets for Chinese porcelain and lacquerware. Society supported literature and the arts.

## PERFORMANCE OBJECTIVES

▶ To analyze the influences of Confucianism

▶ To describe the development of the imperial state and the scholar-official class

▶ To understand the importance of overland trade and maritime expeditions between China and other civilizations

## BUILDING BACKGROUND

Read aloud this sentence from Student Edition page 42: "In Shakespeare's Renaissance England, business was growing, education focused on the classical past, and artists were creating new styles of art. The same was true in Tang Xianzu's [tahng shyen-ZOO's] Ming China." Ask students to predict what will be compared and contrasted in the chapter and then read to confirm their predictions.

## VOCABULARY

**warlord** military ruler of a fairly small area

**dynasty** succession of rulers from the same family line or group

**Confucian ideas** thoughts about the best way to live, developed by the Chinese thinker Confucius and his followers

**hierarchy** structure in which groups are arranged in an order, each more powerful than the one below it

**scholar-official** educated person who held a high position in Chinese government

**neo-Confucianism** revival of Confucius's ideas in the 16th century

## WORKING WITH PRIMARY SOURCES

Read aloud the sidebar on Student Edition page 42. Elicit from students how this poem applies to learning today. Challenge them to restate the message of the poem using a new metaphor.

## GEOGRAPHY CONNECTION

**Regions** On the map of the Ming China on Student Edition page 49, have students infer why the northern border of the Ming dynasty was near the Yellow River. Lead students to understand that the Gobi Desert was most likely a barrier, and it was controlled by the governments of Mongolia and Manchuria.

## READING COMPREHENSION QUESTIONS

1. Which group did Hongwu defeat before becoming emperor? *(the Mongols)*
2. Describe the hierarchy of groups in the Ming society. *(Possible answer: Educated people ruled common people; parents ruled children; men ruled women.)*
3. What topics were covered in the civil service examinations? *(Test topics included Confucian philosophy, law, and literature.)*
4. Why did the Ming emperors extend the Great Wall? *(to keep out the Mongol invaders)*
5. How did culture thrive during the Ming dynasty? *(Artists made porcelain and lacquerware; painters drew upon past traditions and wrote in calligraphy; scholars wrote philosophy, poetry, history, and short stories.)*

## CRITICAL THINKING QUESTIONS

1. Why did Hongwu adopt Confucian beliefs? *(He wanted a well-ordered hierarchy, and Confucian beliefs supported that form of society.)*
2. Read the sidebar on Student Edition page 53. What is the author's point of view? *(The author believes that people should be satisfied with what they have, and that happiness is a state of mind.)*
3. How did contact with European merchants benefit China? *(Spanish and Portuguese merchants brought new crops, which provided nourishment to the growing population. Chinese rulers grew wealthier through trade in porcelain and other desirable goods.)*
4. What is *The Monkey King*? What is its significance? *(It is a funny, magical adventure about a Chinese monk who travels to India in search of Buddhist holy books. The story weaves actual historical events with fantasy; it has been read and performed in a variety of formats through the present day.)*

## SOCIAL SCIENCES

**Civics** Point out that after Hongwu became emperor, he tightened the bureaucracy, wrote a code of laws, and took censuses. He wanted absolute control for himself and the emperors who followed. Have students use library and media connections to research how bureaucracy functioned in the Ming dynasty and create a detailed diagram.

## READING AND LANGUAGE ARTS

**Reading Nonfiction** The chapter compares and contrasts Renaissance Europe and Ming China. Have students find details that show similarities and differences between these two eras.

**Using Language** Direct students to the idiom *broken heart* on Student Edition page 41. Point out that an idiom is an expression whose meaning cannot be inferred from the meanings of the words that make it up. Ask students how they can figure out what this phrase means, based on the context. Encourage them to collect more idioms as they read.

---

### THEN and NOW

Confucianism is a philosophy, and is often called a religion, but there are no Confucian priests or temples. Followers study Confucian writings to guide their lives. Today there are about 6 million people in China who call themselves Confucianists, and many more follow its concepts.

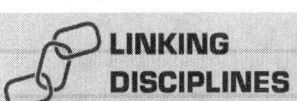

### LINKING DISCIPLINES

**Art** Students can choose a style of art from the Ming dynasty, such as porcelain, calligraphy, or lacquerware, and explain how it reflects Chinese society. Tell them to create a poster to accompany an oral presentation. Direct them to such sites as *www.metmuseum.org/toah/hd/ming/hd_ming.htm*. Use the activity to assess students' understanding of life in Ming China.

AN AGE OF VOYAGES, 1350–1600

## LITERATURE CONNECTION

There are numerous enjoyable books that will broaden students' knowledge of Ming China.

Bosse, Malcolm. *The Examination.* New York: Farrar, Straus and Giroux, 1994. Historical Fiction. Two brothers become involved in the politics of Ming China when one of them earns the right to take an examination with other scholars in Beijing's Forbidden City. AVERGE

Napoli, Donna Jo. *Bound.* New York: Atheneum, 2004. Historical Fiction. Elements of the Chinese Cinderella story shine through this story of a girl's life in Ming China. AVERAGE

Wu, Ch'Eng-En, and Arthur Waley (translator). *Monkey: Folk Novel of China.* London: Grove Press, 1994. Folk Tale. This famed folk tale tells the story of a monk's journey to the West to bring Buddhist scriptures to China. AVERAGE

## LITERACY TIPS

In addition to using the suggestions in the Supporting Learning and Extending Learning sections, refer back frequently to pages 16–19 for strategies and advice from a literacy coach.

## WRITING

**Write a Description** Ask students to imagine that they are Chinese painters during the Ming period. Invite them to describe a painting that reveals their personality. Some students may also wish to accompany their description with a brief poem.

## SUPPORTING LEARNING

**English Language Learners** Use pantomime, realia, and illustrations to help students read and understand the Confucian instruction manual on Student Edition pages 46–47. Ask questions to monitor comprehension based on students' fluency level, and work with students to develop a summary statement for each rule.

**Struggling Readers** Have students list the achievements or features of the Ming dynasty and create a chart to categorize them as *military, economic, government,* or *culture.*

## EXTENDING LEARNING

**Enrichment** Encourage students to read an adventure from *Journey to the West,* or *The Monkey King.* They can read an excerpt at www.china-on-site.com/monkey.php or a summary at www.wku.edu/~yuanh/China/monkey.html. Challenge them to illustrate it as a comic strip.

**Extension** Invite students to create inspirational posters for your school based on Confucian ideas. Suggest that they choose sayings that are relevant to students today, and restate them in conversational language.

NAME _____ DATE _____

# MISS MANNERS

**Directions**

The following text is from *The Medieval & Early Modern World Primary Sources and Reference Volume*, pages 58–59. In it, Miss Zheng describes how women should behave. Read the excerpt with a partner, and answer the questions that follow. If necessary, check a dictionary or use context clues for help with unfamiliar words.

> Lady Ban said . . . "Filial piety expands heaven and earth, deepens human relationships, stimulates the ghosts and spirits, and moves the birds and beasts. It involves being respectful and conforming to ritual, acting only after repeated thought, making no effort to broadcast one's accomplishments or good deeds, being agreeable, gentle, pure, obedient, kind, intelligent, filial, and compassionate. When such virtuous conduct is perfected, no one will reproach you." . . .
>
> *The Common People*
> "They follow the way of the wife and utilize moral principle to the best advantage. They put others first and themselves last in order to serve their parents-in-law. They spin and weave and sew clothes; they prepare the sacrificial foods. This is the filial piety of the wife of a common person." . . .

1. Who is the audience of this guidebook? How can you tell?

2. What were the duties of common women? How could you verify the information?

3. How can you tell that these guidelines are based on Confucian principles?

4. How might following these guidelines contribute to an orderly society?

5. Write a response to the author stating how her beliefs are similar to or different from your own.

# YOUNG PEOPLE SHOULD KNOW THEIR PLACE

**Directions**

This excerpt is from an instructional manual written by a Confucian elder in the late 16th century. It also appears on Student Edition pages 46–47. Read the excerpt, and answer the questions that follow with a partner.

Exercise restraint

1. Our young people should know their place and observe correct manners. They are not permitted to gamble, to fight, to engage in lawsuits, or to deal in salt privately. Such unlawful acts will only lead to their own downfall.

3. Pride is a dangerous trait. Those who pride themselves on wealth, rank, or learning are inviting evil consequences. Even if one's accomplishments are indeed unique, there is no need to press them on anyone else.

5. Just as diseases are caused by what goes into one's mouth, misfortunes are caused by what comes out of one's mouth. Those who are immoderate in eating and unrestrained in speaking have no one else to blame for their own ruin.

**1.** How does the author believe people should exercise, or behave with, restraint?

**2.** What can you tell about the problems in Ming society, based on the saying that begins "Our young people . . . "?

**3.** Restate one of the sayings in your own words. Did you state an opinion or a fact? How can you tell?

**4.** Think about what you read about the original Confucian beliefs. How can you tell that ancient Confucian ideas had an effect on this author?

**NAME**                          **DATE**

## A. MULTIPLE CHOICE

**Circle the letter of the best answer to each question.**

1. Which is not an important similarity between William Shakespeare and Tang Xianzu?
   a. They were jailed for their revolutionary ideas.
   b. They wrote plays that were eventually made into movies.
   c. They updated old stories with fresh language.
   d. They were from middle-class backgrounds.

2. How can you tell that Emperor Yongle valued knowledge and scholarship?
   a. He became the first neo-Confucianist.
   b. He set up the first civil service examinations.
   c. He paid for thousands of writers to compile an encyclopedia.
   d. He gave financial support to Confucius.

3. What is the main reason why Confucius developed his ideas?
   a. He wanted to give commoners more opportunities.
   b. He wanted to open China to the outside world.
   c. He wanted to give women more opportunities.
   d. He wanted society to be more peaceful.

4. What goods or products did China originally import from European traders?
   a. peanuts and corn
   b. porcelain plates and bowls
   c. lacquerware boxes and chests
   d. paintings with calligraphy

5. What is the title of the popular adventure story about a Chinese monk?
   a. *The Peony Pavilion*
   b. *The Golden Lotus*
   c. *The Monkey King*
   d. *Analects*

## B. SHORT ANSWER

**Answer each question with one or more sentences.**

6. How can you tell that Hongwu did not respect the former Mongol rulers? Give examples.

7. Describe women's roles under the Confucian concept of the "Three Obediences."

8. How did civil service examinations benefit commoners?

9. How did trade with foreigners affect China? Give examples.

## C. MAKING COMPARISONS

**Write an essay on a separate sheet of paper explaining how Renaissance Europe and Ming China were similar.**

# CHAPTER 4

# BLACK AND WHITE AND READ ALL OVER: THE PRINTING PRESS
## PAGES 54–68

**FOR HOMEWORK**

Student Study Guide pages 23–26

**CAST OF CHARACTERS**

**Gutenberg** (GOO-ten-burg), **Johan** (YO-hahn) German goldsmith, inventor of the printing press

**Erasmus** (eh-RAHS-mus), **Desiderius** (deh-she-DEHR-ee-us) Dutch humanist, scholar, and author

**Luther, Martin** German religious reformer who began the Protestant Reformation

### CHAPTER SUMMARY

Around 1450 in Germany, Johan Gutenberg invented a printing press with movable type. Prior to this invention, each page in a book had to be copied by hand or carved in a single block of wood. This work-intensive process meant that books were very expensive and rare. Gutenberg's invention changed the world, making books, and thus education and mass culture, widely available.

### PERFORMANCE OBJECTIVES

- To identify Johan Gutenberg as the inventor of movable type
- To compare and contrast earlier printing methods with those of Gutenberg
- To understand how the printing press led Europe to develop mass culture

### BUILDING BACKGROUND

Work with students to brainstorm a list of modern means of communication, including text-based methods such as hand-written notes, e-mail, websites, and text messaging. Then ask groups to cross out communication methods that require machines or technology. Tell students that they will read about the invention of a machine that changed the way people learned and shared ideas.

### VOCABULARY

**professionals** skilled workers, such as doctors, accountants, and authors

**movable type** metal letters that could be rearranged and reused to form words

**craft guild** an organization of skilled workers

**copyright** legal protection against copying and theft of a person's original work

**mass culture** ideas that are widely available to many people

As needed, have students consult the glossary to define the following words: *bestiary, block-book, journeyman, printer's devil, type.*

### WORKING WITH PRIMARY SOURCES

Point out the quotation from David Hume on Student Edition page 66, and discuss its implications with students. Have students speculate about why Hume might have thought of the printing process as an art.

### GEOGRAPHY CONNECTION

**Location** Use the world map on Student Edition pages 10–11 to have students locate Germany, where Johan Gutenberg invented his printing press, and China and Korea, where woodblock printing and movable type had been used hundreds of years earlier. Discuss how the distances between the locations, as well as geography, modes of transportation, and societal differences, affected communication.

## READING COMPREHENSION QUESTIONS

1. Why was Gutenberg's invention called "movable" type? (*Each piece of type was a single letter, which could be arranged with other letters to form words. Each piece of type could be moved and used again and again.*)

2. Why were books both rare and expensive before Gutenberg's invention? (*Each book was handwritten, or printed by carving the words and sentences into wood.*)

3. Why did government and church leaders attempt to censor certain books? (*They feared that a large number of copies of books containing controversial ideas could influence what people thought of the government or the church.*)

4. In Gutenberg's time, what steps might a young man take to become a printer? (*He would contract himself to a master printer as an apprentice and work for five to ten years learning the craft. Then he would become a journeyman, working as an assistant to a master printer for another five to ten years. Then he would prove his abilities by printing a "masterpiece." If other printers found it acceptable, he would be considered a master printer, capable of opening his own shop.*)

## CRITICAL THINKING QUESTIONS

1. Thanks to Gutenberg's press, Europe gained mass culture for the first time. What were the benefits of mass culture? (*People had equal access to the same information, art, music, and entertainment, regardless of social class and economics. People also had access to different ways of thinking.*)

2. In 2001, a cable-television network cited Gutenberg as being the most influential person of the previous 1,000 years. What facts might have led to their choice? (*His invention allowed for the mass production of books and newspapers. It furthered the power of written language. It literally changed the way people communicated and learned.*)

3. How is a modern computer keyboard like Gutenberg's movable type? How is it different? (*Like Gutenberg's type, a keyboard allows the user to put individual letters together in an infinite number of combinations to form words; each letter can be used over and over again. A keyboard is different in that it does not involve solid pieces of metal that have to be physically moved and set together; using a keyboard to fix errors is easier and faster.*)

## SOCIAL SCIENCES

**Economics** Have students work in small groups to discuss how the spread of print shops provided jobs beyond the print shops themselves. If necessary, prompt their thinking by pointing out that printers had to purchase ink from an outside merchant, and that books produced were bought and sold. Allow time for groups to summarize their discussions for the class. Use the activity to assess students' understanding of the far-reaching impact of the invention of the printing press.

---

### THEN and NOW

Gutenberg was able to print 300 copies of a single page in one day, which people saw as a miracle. And it was miraculous, compared to the laborious process of copying entire books by hand. A modern laser printer can print 8 pages of text per minute, or 480 pages per hour.

### 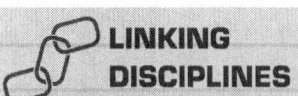 LINKING DISCIPLINES

**Art** Students might enjoy creating pages similar to the page from the Gutenberg Bible shown on Student Edition page 57. Have them experiment with different fonts on available word processors. Then encourage them to use paints, markers, or colored pencils to add embellishments.

---

AN AGE OF VOYAGES, 1350–1600

## LITERATURE CONNECTION

There are numerous enjoyable books that will broaden students' knowledge of the impact of the printing press on the medieval world.

Crompton, Samuel Willard. *The Printing Press: Transforming Power of Technology.* New York: Chelsea House, 2003. Nonfiction. Crompton examines the invention that changed civilization. AVERAGE

Tames, Richard. *The Printing Press: A Breakthrough in Communication.* Chicago: Heinemann Library, 2001. Nonfiction. From Asia to Europe, printing changed the medieval world. EASY

Vernon, Louise. *Ink on His Fingers.* Severna Park, MD: Greenleaf Press, 1993. Historical Fiction. An apprentice becomes involved in a mystery as he helps Gutenberg print the Bible. EASY

## LITERACY TIPS

In addition to using the suggestions in the Supporting Learning and Extending Learning sections, refer back frequently to pages 16–19 for strategies and advice from a literacy coach.

## READING AND LANGUAGE ARTS

**Reading Nonfiction** Have students use text features such as headings, subheadings, and captions along with the images shown to summarize the main points in the chapter.

**Using Language** Point out compound words such as *masterpiece, copyright,* and *proofread* in the chapter and have students scan the text for additional examples. Discuss how the meanings of the smaller words in each compound contribute to its meaning. Then have students research the words' origins further using an etymology dictionary or an online resources such as *www.etymonline.com*.

## WRITING

**Summary** Have students write summaries of "Black and White and Read All Over." Remind them to include the chapter's main ideas and most important details and to use quotation marks if they choose to use the author's exact words as part of their summaries.

## SUPPORTING LEARNING

**English Language Learners** Explain or elicit that some English words have more than one meaning. Then lead them to understand the specialized meanings used on Student Edition page 54 for the words *mint, type,* and *press*.

**Struggling Readers** To help students understand the concept of movable type, have them print single letters on index cards and then rearrange the letters to form simple words. For example, have them print the letters *c, a, r,* and *e*. Work with them to arrange the letters to form the word *care*. Then have them rearrange them to form *race* and *acre*. Another simple combination is *e, d, i, t* (*edit, diet, tied, tide*).

## EXTENDING LEARNING

**Enrichment** Have students use library or Internet resources to find simple directions for making and processing paper pulp. You may wish to suggest *www.pioneerthinking.com/makingpaper.html*. Then have them work in small groups to make their paper and then print messages. They might use letters on rubber stamps to simulate Gutenberg's use of movable type.

**Extension** Have students list and discuss various forms of "mass culture" that Europeans shared for the first time, thanks to Gutenberg's invention. Invite them to create a bulletin board display comparing mass culture in Gutenberg's time with modern culture.

# THE ROOTS OF EUROPEAN MASS CULTURE, 1500

**Directions**

Reread this passage from Student Edition page 58. Then follow the directions below to show on the map how printing spread through Europe between 1450 and 1500.

> Soon after Gutenberg began printing, other craftsmen made their own type, built their own presses, and bought their own paper, setting themselves up for business in cities in Germany, Switzerland, and the Netherlands, and then in Italy, England, and France. By 1480, about 110 cities in Europe had presses. Printing continued to spread to Spain and Scandinavia, and by 1500, roughly 50 years after the first books were printed, more than 200 cities and towns in Europe had presses.

- ▶ Use a colored pencil to highlight the country in which Gutenberg developed his press with movable type at about 1450.
- ▶ Use a second colored pencil to highlight the countries in which presses were established by 1480.
- ▶ Use a third colored pencil to highlight the countries in which presses were established between 1480 and 1500.
- ▶ Create a legend for your map to show what each color indicates.

**NAME**                                    **DATE**

## COUNT ROLAND'S LAST STAND

**Directions**

The following text is from a letter written by Desiderius Erasmus, which appears in *The Medieval & Early Modern World Primary Sources and Reference Volume*, pages 90–91. In the letter, written in 1513, he shares his ideas about war. Read the passage. Then, with a partner, answer the questions that follow.

> We spend our whole lives fighting wars. Not even animals do that, except wild ones, and they do not battle with their own kind, but only with members of a different species; they fight with the weapons with which nature provided them, not like us, with war machinery devised by the devil's art. Nor do they fight for any and every reason, but only to protect their young and get food, while our wars, for the most part, are the result of ambition or anger or lust or some such disease of the soul. Finally, animals do not mass together by the thousands, as we do, and then line up to destroy each other.

**1.** In your own words, summarize Erasmus's point of view about war. Do you agree with him? Explain why or why not.

_____
_____
_____
_____

**2.** In Chapter 4, you learned that some people felt that printing was "the devil's invention." In this letter, Erasmus suggests that weapons of war are "devised by the devil's art." Why might people have connected each of these technologies to the devil?

_____
_____
_____
_____

**3.** Erasmus makes some generalizations about what motivates animals to fight and people to start wars. Restate his generalizations in your own words. Do you think they are fair and accurate generalizations? Explain.

_____
_____
_____
_____

**4.** Think back on what you learned in Chapter 4 about the establishment of mass culture in Europe. How might the printing press have led people to "mass together by the thousands" and then "line up to destroy each other"?

_____
_____
_____
_____

**NAME**                      **DATE**

## A. MULTIPLE CHOICE

**Circle the letter of the best answer for each question.**

1. Gutenberg's method of printing was new and different because
   a. each page was carved out of wood.
   b. it used ceramic type, like that developed in Korea.
   c. it used movable type, one block for each letter in a word.
   d. it used movable type, one block for each word in a sentence.

2. What is the best definition of a craft guild?
   a. a market where craftsmen could gather to sell their goods
   b. a manual, or guide, explaining how to make various crafts
   c. an organization that made printed copies of all laws so that they would not be lost
   d. an organization that made rules about the training and protection of craftsmen

3. Which of the following generalizations is fair and accurate, based on the facts presented in Chapter 4?
   a. Gutenberg's press eventually led to widespread illiteracy.
   b. Gutenberg's press eventually led to European mass culture.
   c. Gutenberg's press involved secret technology that was difficult to copy.
   d. Gutenberg's press used many different colors of ink.

4. Before Europeans learned how to make paper, books were very expensive because
   a. they required the processing of linen and hemp.
   b. members of the clergy often read them aloud to the mostly illiterate peasants.
   c. government and religious leaders confiscated books that they judged as "dangerous."
   d. they were printed on sheepskin or calfskin, which were both very costly.

## B. SHORT ANSWER

**Answer these questions in two or three sentences.**

5. What did a journeyman have to do to become a master craftsman?

6. What was the purpose of copyright laws?

## C. WRITING

On a separate sheet of paper, write a persuasive essay to give your opinion about the efforts to censor books or authors by government or church leaders, as described in Chapter 4. Are such efforts always wrong? Are there situations in which censorship is useful? Explain and support your opinion.

# CHAPTER 5

# LUTHER, LOYOLA, MOBS, AND MASSACRES: THE PROTESTANT AND CATHOLIC REFORMATIONS  PAGES 69–8

**FOR HOMEWORK**
Student Study Guide pages 27–30

## CHAPTER SUMMARY

In 1521, a monk named Martin Luther rebelled against the Catholic Church. In a few decades, most of central and northern Europe had split from the Catholic Church in a movement called the Protestant Reformation. The reformers used the printing press to spread their ideas. The Catholic Church responded by initiating its own reforms and combating the spread of Protestantism. The cultural unrest led to more than a century of religious wars.

## PERFORMANCE OBJECTIVES

- To list the causes for the weakening of the Catholic Church
- To describe the contributions of the major figures during the Reformation
- To understand the impact of missionaries on Christianity

## BUILDING BACKGROUND

Direct students to brainstorm words and phrases associated with the Catholic Church in medieval Europe. Tell them that in this chapter, they will learn how Protestant reformers broke from the Catholic Church, and what happened as a result. Remind them that as they read, they should look for events that caused other events to happen.

**CAST OF CHARACTERS**

**Tyndale** (TIHN-duhl), **William** English religious reformer and translator of the Bible

**Calvin, John** French Protestant religious reformer

**Loyola** (loy-OH-lah), **Ignatius** (ig-NAY-shus) Spanish Catholic religious reformer, founder of the Jesuits

## VOCABULARY

**pacifist** a person who is opposed to war or violence to resolve disputes
**persecution** the act of oppressing someone based on his or her beliefs
**missionary** one sent to do religious work in a territory or foreign country

## WORKING WITH PRIMARY SOURCES

Read aloud the sidebar on page 77. Ask students to describe the mood of the quotation, the context in which it was stated, and how it might have been a call to action for supporters of Michael Sattler.

## GEOGRAPHY CONNECTION

**Interaction** Have students locate the German Empire on the map on Student Edition page 82 and list the religions practiced within its borders. Have them speculate why it was not unified under one religion, as in the nearby countries of France or Spain.

CHAPTER 5

## READING COMPREHENSION QUESTIONS

1. Why did Martin Luther criticize the pope and bishops? (*He felt that they had too much power and that they were more interested in money than in faith.*)

2. Why wasn't Martin Luther arrested as a heretic? (*The emperor of Germany did not want soldiers to enter Saxony to arrest Luther, and the pope was concerned by the situation with the Ottoman Turks.*)

3. What forms of mass media did reformers use to spread their ideas? (*inexpensive illustrated booklets and posters*)

4. How did rulers benefit by breaking from the Catholic Church? (*Rulers could confiscate the church's land and property and have more control over people's lives.*)

5. Why did the king of France declare a truce between Calvinists and Catholics in 1598? (*There was too much warfare, riots, and assassinations on both sides.*)

## CRITICAL THINKING QUESTIONS

1. How can you tell that radicals were viewed as a serious threat? (*Many were persecuted, tortured, and executed.*)

2. How can you tell that the author of the textbook believes that some women were tried unjustly as witches? (*The author states that printed pamphlets fueled the hysteria against so-called witches, and that the evidence against the accused women was often exaggerated.*)

3. How did pacifists interpret the Bible phrase "turn the other cheek"? (*They believed it meant that they should not fight in wars.*)

4. How were the Jesuits able to stop the further spread of Protestant ideas in some places? (*They set up schools, taught at universities, preached popular sermons, and worked as missionaries.*)

## SOCIAL SCIENCES

**Civics** Point out that since government and religion were closely allied in medieval times, both religious and civic leaders were affected by the turmoil of the Protestant Reformation. Governments based on religious practices, or theocracies, have existed since ancient times. Have volunteers research a modern theocracy such as Iran or Vatican City, and prepare an oral report.

## READING AND LANGUAGE ARTS

**Reading Nonfiction** The chapter describes how individuals such as Martin Luther and John Calvin changed religious beliefs and shaped cultures and societies. Have students create and complete a three-column chart with the headings *Reformer, Beliefs,* and *Influences or Changes*. Guide students to use the chart to summarize the chapter. Use the activity to assess students' understanding of the impact of the Protestant Reformation.

**Using Language** Direct students to the word *brutal* on Student Edition page 81 and discuss its denotation (literal meaning) and connotation (implied meaning). Elicit that using a word with a strong connotation can affect the reader's mood. Have students choose a quotation or passage and analyze the use of words that have positive or negative connotations.

AN AGE OF VOYAGES, 1350–1600

---

### THEN and NOW

In the 1500s Jesuit missionaries worked in Brazil, Mexico, India, and Japan. Christian missionaries today work in such countries as Vietnam, Bangladesh, Brazil, Malta, Sri Lanka, Trinidad, and Uganda.

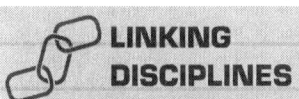

### LINKING DISCIPLINES

**Science** Suggest to students that they view political cartoons from the time of the Protestant Reformation at such sites as *http://xroads.virginia.edu/~MA96/PUCK/part1.html*. Then have them draw an original political cartoon that might have appeared in a pamphlet during this era. Remind them to use persuasive techniques.

## LITERATURE CONNECTION

### LITERATURE CONNECTION

There are numerous enjoyable books that will broaden students' knowledge of the changes brought about by the Protestant and Catholic reformations.

De Wohl, Louis. *The Golden Thread: A Novel About St. Ignatius Loyola.* Harrison, NY: Ignatius Press, 2002. Historical Fiction. The early life of Ignatius Loyola is at the center of this novel.
ADVANCED

Crompton, Samuel Willard. *Martin Luther.* New York: Chelsea House, 2004. Biography. The author examines the challenges, contradictions, and commitment of the man credited with bringing about the Protestant Reformation.
AVERAGE

## LITERACY TIPS

In addition to using the suggestions in the Supporting Learning and Extending Learning sections, refer back frequently to pages 16–19 for strategies and advice from a literacy coach.

## WRITING

**Narrative** Ask students to choose a person from the chapter and write a fictional narrative based on real events in that person's life. They may wish to conduct additional research before writing their drafts.

## SUPPORTING LEARNING

**English Language Learners** Work with students to list religious terms and their meanings in their history journals. You may wish to prompt them with words from the chapter such as *faith, prayer, saints, Bible, monasteries, sermons,* and *baptism*. Have them read aloud the definitions and answer questions about each term.

**Struggling Readers** Suggest that students ask themselves questions to make connections. Model the concept with questions such as: *What have I read that reminds me of other current or historical conflicts? How are the conflicts similar? How are they different?*

## EXTENDING LEARNING

**Enrichment** Have students use an encyclopedia and other library resources to research and compare the religious persecution of people accused of witchcraft in Europe and in the North American colonies. Allow time for students to report to the class what they learned.

**Extension** Direct small groups of students to imagine they are city leaders in Geneva in the 1560s. Have them hold a debate in which they argue for or against reforming the government, based on John Calvin's proposals.

NAME                    DATE

## EUROPE AFTER THE REFORMATION, 1580

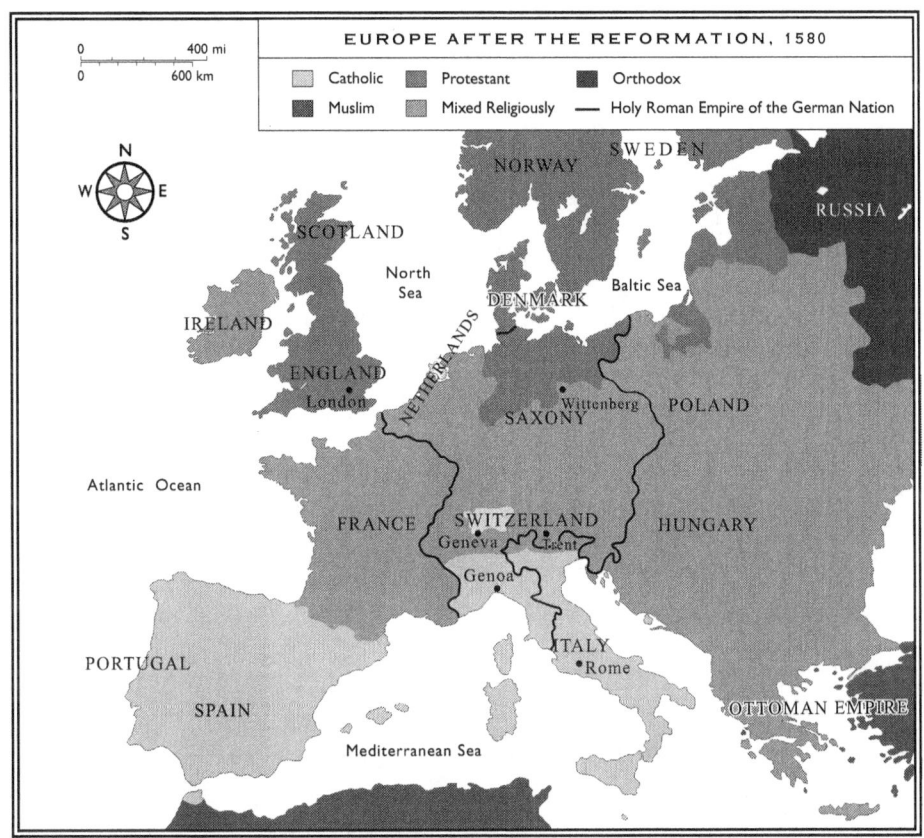

**Directions**

Use the map to answer the questions that follow.

1. What country practiced the Orthodox religion?

2. Describe where Martin Luther's religious beliefs spread, starting in Wittenberg.

3. What is the dominant religion in Italy, Spain, and Portugal?

4. In what areas might you have found continued religious conflicts? Why?

5. How can you tell that more than one religion was practiced in the Ottoman Empire?

**NAME** _____  **DATE** _____

# THE SOUL NEEDS ONLY THE WORD OF GOD

**Directions**

This excerpt is from a brief pamphlet titled *The Freedom of a Christian*, written by Martin Luther in 1520. It also appears on Student Edition page 73. Read the excerpt and, with a partner, answer the questions that follow.

> What can it profit the soul if the body is well, free, and active, and eats, drinks, and does what it pleases? For in these respects even the most godless slave of vice may prosper. On the other hand, how will poor health or imprisonment or hunger or thirst or any other external misfortune harm the soul? Even the most godly men . . . are afflicted with these things. None of these things touches either the freedom or the servitude of the soul. . . . One thing, and only one thing, is necessary for Christian life, righteousness, and freedom. That one thing is the most holy Word of God, the gospel of Christ . . . as the soul needs only the Word of God for its life and righteousness, so it is justified by faith alone and not any works. . . . But as long as he lives in the flesh . . . and remains in this mortal life on earth . . . a man cannot be idle, for his body drives him and he is compelled to do many good works to reduce it to subjection [that is, to make sure his desire for power, money, fame, food, or other earthly things does not take over his life]. Nevertheless the works themselves do not justify him before God, but he does works out of spontaneous love in obedience to God.

**1.** Why do you think Martin Luther wrote this pamphlet?

_____
_____
_____

**2.** What does he believe about the souls of people who are healthy but godless?

_____
_____
_____

**3.** What does he believe about the souls of people who are religious but in poor health?

_____
_____
_____

**4.** Why does Martin Luther believe that people should do good works?

_____
_____
_____

**5.** Why do you think Martin Luther's words had a lasting effect on people?

_____
_____
_____

# CHAPTER TEST 5

**An Age of Voyages, 1350–1600**

## A. MULTIPLE CHOICE

**Circle the letter of the best answer for each question.**

1. Which was **not** one of the Protestant reformers' main criticisms?
   a. Magical practices like baptizing magnets should not be part of church practices.
   b. The pope's headquarters should be moved from Rome to Germany.
   c. The church should give up its wealth.
   d. The religious services should be in languages people spoke.

2. How were Martin Luther, William Tyndale, and John Calvin similar?
   a. They were executed for their beliefs.
   b. They started Jesuit schools.
   c. They protested against the Catholic hierarchy.
   d. They became radical pacifists.

3. What was the effect of the truce following France's religious warfare?
   a. France remained Catholic but allowed Protestants certain freedoms.
   b. France became Catholic and forced Protestants to leave the country.
   c. France had no official religion.
   d. France became Protestant and forced Catholics to convert.

4. Who defeated the Spanish Armada in 1588?
   a. the Portuguese    c. the French
   b. the Germans       d. the English

## B. CAUSE AND EFFECT

**Write one or two short sentences to answer the following questions.**

| CAUSE | EFFECT |
| --- | --- |
| 5. | Radicals moved to places where the rulers were more tolerant. |
| 6. | People in Geneva had to go to a special new court if they were accused of gambling or fighting. |
| 7 | Teresa of Avila reformed and reorganized convents in Spain. |
| 8. | The Catholic Church leaders held the Council of Trent, which reestablished Catholic beliefs. |

## C. MAKING INFERENCES

Why do you think the founders of the United States made religious freedom a right for all citizens? Write an essay on a separate sheet of paper explaining your ideas. Include historical evidence from the chapter.

# CHAPTER 6
## "ASTONISHING," "MAGNIFICENT," "GREAT": RULERS AND RELIGION IN EUROPE AND ASIA  PAGES 84–96

**FOR HOMEWORK**

Student Study Guide pages 31–34

**CAST OF CHARACTERS**

**Suleyman** (soo-lay-mahn), **the Magnificent** Ottoman sultan

**Isabella of Castile** queen of Spain

**Ferdinand of Aragon** king of Spain

**Selim "the Grim"** Ottoman sultan, father of Suleyman, effective military leader

**Akbar** (AK-bahr) Mughal emperor and religious reformer

**Babur** (BAH-bur) founder of the Mughal Empire, grandfather of Akbar

## CHAPTER SUMMARY

The Ottoman Empire grew during the 16th century under the reigns of Sultan Selim "the Grim" and his son, Suleyman. At about the same time, the Mughal Empire in northern India also grew in size and power, under the rulers Babur and his grandson, Akbar. Both empires strove to unite their empires through religious tolerance. On the Iberian Peninsula, however, religious intolerance under Ferdinand and Isabella led to the Spanish Inquisition and the expulsion of Jews, and later, Muslims.

## PERFORMANCE OBJECTIVES

▶ To understand the expansion of Muslim rule in the Ottoman Empire

▶ To explain the decline of Muslim rule on the Iberian Peninsula as Christian rulers controlled Spain and Portugal

▶ To describe the Spanish Inquisition and the persecution and expulsion of Jews and Muslims from Spain

▶ To understand the growth of the Mughal Empire

## BUILDING BACKGROUND

Ask students to identify the religions that are practiced in the United States, and create a list of their responses. Lead a discussion about the separation of religion and government in this country, as mandated by our Constitution. Tell students that Chapter 6 discusses the how religion played both unifying and divisive roles in empires in Europe and Asia.

## VOCABULARY

**bureaucracy** system run by officials appointed by government leaders

**convert** to adopt a different religion

**religious diversity** a variety of different religions or beliefs

**hostile** feeling or showing a deep-seated hatred

**scapegoats** people or groups bearing blame for others

**tolerance** the ability to allow or respect the beliefs or behavior of others

As needed, have students consult the glossary to define the following words: *gunpowder empire, Janissaries, vizier.*

## WORKING WITH PRIMARY SOURCES

Point out the photograph of the Suleymaniye mosque on Student Edition page 84. Explain that its architect, Sinan, had been a construction officer in the Ottoman army and went on to design hundreds of building projects for the Ottoman Empire. Have students use print or electronic references to learn more about Sinan, his influences, and his vast body of work.

## GEOGRAPHY CONNECTION

**Location** Have students look at the map on page 86. Point out that Suleiman brought Croatia, Romania, Bosnia, and most of the Ukraine into the Ottoman Empire during the 16th century. Discuss the geographic reasons that the Ottomans engaged in sea battles with Italian trading cities.

## READING COMPREHENSION QUESTIONS

1. How did the Ottoman Empire expand during the 14th century? How did Ottoman sultans differ in their rule from European leaders? (*The Ottoman Empire conquered lands beyond what is now Turkey to the east and parts of Europe in the west. Ottoman rulers allowed conquered people to follow their own laws, traditions, and religious beliefs, unlike European rulers.*)

2. How did rule of the Iberian Peninsula change between the 8th and 13th centuries? (*Muslims controlled the Iberian Peninsula for many centuries, but by the late 1200s, Christian rulers had taken over all of these lands, except for Granada.*)

3. What were the results of the Spanish Inquisition? (*Many people were persecuted and executed, and by the end of the 15th century, all Jews and Muslims were forced to leave Spain.*)

4. How were the rulers Suleyman and Akbar alike? How were they different? (*Both used religious tolerance to unify their lands, but Akbar was especially interested in developing religious tolerance to bring social harmony.*)

5. What were some of the religions that coexisted in the Mughal Empire under Akbar? (*Islam, Hinduism, Christianity, Judaism, Zoroastrianism, Jainism, and Sikhism*)

## CRITICAL THINKING QUESTIONS

1. How did laws controlling Jewish people in Europe lead to prejudice and persecution? (*Jews could not own property, so they became bankers and traders, and the special privileges they received for these services caused others to resent them.*)

2. Why do you think Christian subjects cooperated in providing Janissaries for Turkish troops? (*They really had no choice, but perhaps saw it as a way to improve their children's lives.*)

3. Why do you think Muslims would not support Akbar's Divine Faith? (*Akbar's Divine Faith included worship of Akbar, which went directly against Muslim beliefs.*)

4. Several religions coexisted in the Mughal Empire under Akbar. Why do you think this was so? (*Possible answer: Akbar believed that tolerance for different religions would promote justice and harmony to his empire, and would increase support for his rule.*)

## SOCIAL SCIENCES

**Science, Technology, and Society** The invention of gunpowder marked a profound change in how battles were fought. Encourage students to learn more about this singular invention and its impact on military strategy and technology. Ask volunteers to share their findings in an oral report.

---

### THEN and NOW

For centuries, India's caste system included a large group known as untouchables, who performed jobs that no one else would do. In 1950, the Indian constitution gave the group full citizenship and outlawed untouchability. However, discrimination against this group, now called dalits, has not been completely eradicated.

### LINKING DISCIPLINES

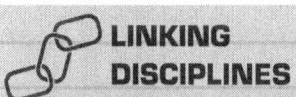

**Art** Encourage students to use library resources and the Internet to learn more about the thinking behind Islamic visual arts, including the avoidance of representations of living things. Students may find *http://en.wikipedia.org/wiki/Islamic_art_history* a helpful starting point for their research. Have volunteers present their findings in oral reports accompanied by relevant visuals.

AN AGE OF VOYAGES, 1350–1600

## LITERATURE CONNECTION

There are numerous enjoyable books that will broaden students' knowledge of the Mughal and Ottoman empires.

Addison, John. *Suleyman and the Ottoman Empire.* San Diego: Greenhaven Press, 1986. Biography. The life of the leader who reigned during the golden age of the Ottoman Empire is the subject of this biography. AVERAGE

Findly, Ellison Banks. *Nur Jahn: Empress of Mughal India.* New York: Oxford University Press, 1993. Biography. This account details the life of one of the most powerful women in Indian history. ADVANCED

Schimmel, Annemarie. *The Empire of the Great Mughals: History, Art, and Culture.* London: Reaktion Books, 2004. Nonfiction. The author examines the cultural and artistic achievements of the Mughal Empire. ADVANCED

## LITERACY TIPS

In addition to using the suggestions in the Supporting Learning and Extending Learning sections, refer back frequently to pages 16–19 for strategies and advice from a literacy coach.

## READING AND LANGUAGE ARTS

**Reading Nonfiction** As this chapter discusses a variety of people, places, and events, tell students to create categories as they read, such as *Leaders, Places,* and *Religions,* and list examples for each category. Students may also find it helpful to compile a list of names and titles along with the translation or meaning of terms. Have pairs or small groups of students compare and discuss their categories. You may also use the activity to assess students' understanding of the chapter content.

**Using Language** Review the writings of a Christian monk on page 88 about the rumors about Jews. Explain that this type of propaganda uses inflammatory language to spread resentment and hatred. Have students identify language in the quotations that served to foster hatred for Jews.

## WRITING

**Interview** Invite students to write a fictitious interview with the sultan Suleyman or with the emperor Akbar to find out why they chose to allow people to follow their own religious beliefs, as opposed to Christian rulers in Europe. Interviews should include at least three questions and responses.

## SUPPORTING LEARNING

**English Language Learners** Work with students to develop awareness of synonyms. For beginning learners, have students identify and practice using synonyms from the chapter such as *astonishing* and *amazing, magnificent* and *great.* Guide students to use a thesaurus to find other synonyms. Have small groups of intermediate and advanced learners locate and use synonyms in the chapter that describe rulers, such as *sultan, emperor,* and *leader.*

**Struggling Readers** Have pairs of students work together to create timelines that tell about the development and expansion of the Ottoman and Mughal Empires. Tell them to use the timeline graphic organizer at the back of this guide. Encourage students to include page numbers that identify where they found information for the events. Invite students to compare their timelines.

## EXTENDING LEARNING

**Enrichment** Encourage students to investigate the religious diversity of today's world. Have pairs or small groups prepare a visual or oral presentation that describes global patterns of religious beliefs.

**Extension** Akbar gathered together people of different faiths for discussions of religion. Have students portray followers of the various religions and discuss how tolerance can build strength and social harmony.

# THE OTTOMAN AND MUGHAL EMPIRES, 1550

**Directions**
Use the map to answer the questions that follow.

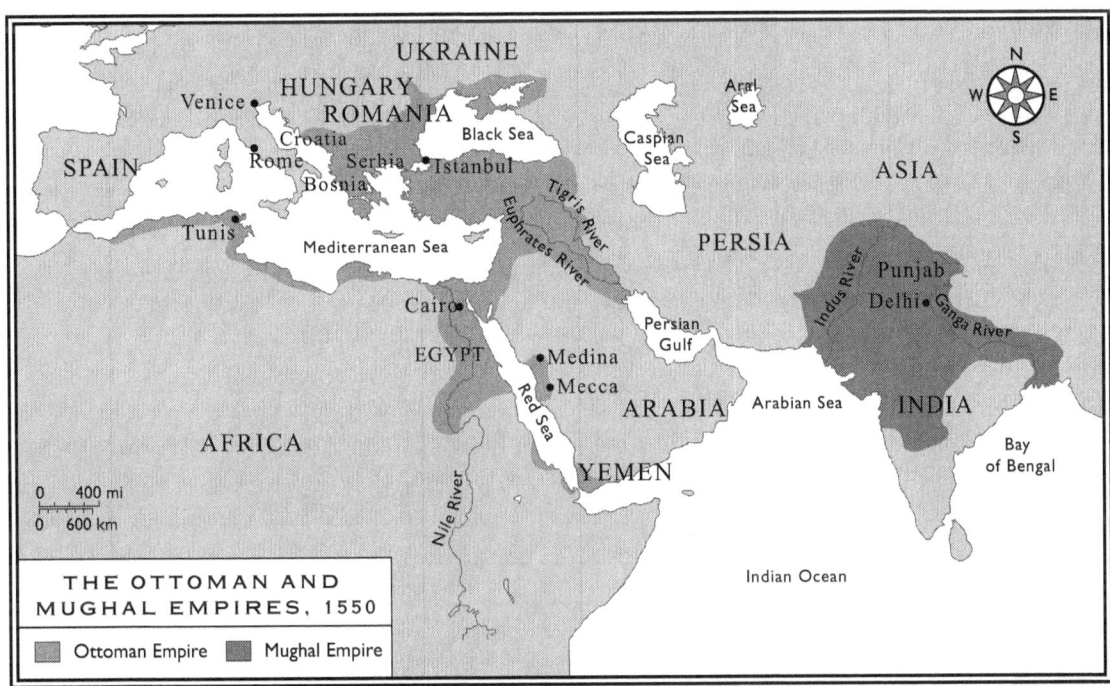

1. Which empire was larger in area?

2. Write a sentence that tells how much of the land surrounding the Mediterranean Sea was controlled by the Ottoman Empire in 1550.

3. Which empire probably controlled the most trade routes in 1550? Explain your answer.

4. Why do you think northern border of the Mughal Empire is near the Indus and Ganga Rivers?

5. Use the scale of miles to tell how far the Ottoman Empire was from the Mughal Empire in 1550.

## THE TRUEST AND MIGHTIEST RELIGION

**Directions**

This excerpt from a speech delivered by the emperor Akbar to religious scholars in 1580 also appears on Student Edition page 94. Read the excerpt, and answer the questions that follow with a partner.

> I perceive that there are varying customs and beliefs of varying religious paths. For the teachings of the Hindus, the Muslims, the Parsis, the Jews, and the Christians are all different. But the followers of each religion regard the institutions of their own religion as better than those of any other. Not only so, but they strive to convert the rest to their own way of belief. If they refuse to be converted, they not only despise them, but also regard them for this very reason as their enemies. And this causes me to feel many serious doubts and scruples. Wherefore I desire that on appointed days the books of all religious laws be brought forward, and the doctors [of the study of religion] meet and hold discussions, so that I may hear them, and that each one may determine which is the truest and mightiest religion.

1. Akbar said, "the followers of each religion regard the institutions of their own religion as better than those of any other." Do you think he believes this is good or bad? Why?

2. What is one reason that Akbar might have chosen to give this speech?

3. Why do you think scholars came to hear Akbar's speech?

4. Why do you think Akbar wants religious scholars to "determine which is the truest and mightiest religion"?

5. Why would it be important to people of Akbar's time that a religion be both true and mighty?

# NAME _____ DATE _____

## A. MULTIPLE CHOICE

**Circle the letter of the best answer for each question.**

1. Under the sultan Suleyman, the Ottoman Empire
    a. became known as a gunpowder empire and was held together primarily through force and religious intolerance.
    b. came to control about a third of Europe and about half of the lands bordering the Mediterranean Sea.
    c. accepted many religious beliefs and encouraged the spread of Hinduism.
    d. lost control of the Iberian Peninsula to Ferdinand and Isabella of Spain.

2. The purpose of the Spanish Inquisition was to
    a. increase the power of the pope.
    b. overthrow Muslim control of the Iberian Peninsula.
    c. conduct fair trials of people suspected of practicing non-Christian religions.
    d. enforce Christian beliefs in Spain.

3. Within the Ottoman Empire, Janissaries
    a. were prisoners of war who collected taxes from Christian subjects.
    b. came from Christian families that refused to convert to Islam and were forced to do the lowest forms of labor.
    c. were Muslim boys chosen to be prepared as viziers to the sultans.
    d. were legally slaves, but could rise to positions of great power.

4. Several of the religions that were brought to or formed within the Mughal Empire
    a. believed in the idea of an eternal soul and felt that all life was sacred.
    b. worked together to force an end to the caste system.
    c. rejected Muslim ideas and worked to drive Muslims from the empire.
    d. disagreed with the emperor Akbar and eventually overthrew him.

5. The emperor Akbar's Divine Faith
    a. successfully united the people of the Mughal Empire for several centuries.
    b. established Hinduism as the official religion of the Mughal Empire.
    c. sought to combine ideas from many religions, with Akbar at its center.
    d. angered many Jews and Christians and united them to revolt against Mughal rule.

## B. SUMMARIZE

Write a summary that tells how the Ottoman and Mughal Empires were alike, and how their policies toward religion contrasted with those of rulers in western Europe at the time. Use the following terms in your summary: *gunpowder empire* and *religious diversity*.

_____
_____
_____
_____
_____
_____
_____
_____

# CHAPTER 7
# GUTS, GAIN, AND GLORY: POWERFUL MONARCHS IN ENGLAND AND AFRICA PAGES 97–108

**FOR HOMEWORK**
Student Study Guide pages 35–38

## CHAPTER SUMMARY

Powerful leaders—Elizabeth I, Sunni Ali Ber, Askia the Great, and Afonso I—left their mark on the 15th and 16th centuries. Elizabeth I stabilized England in the aftermath of her father's chaotic reign, and made her country a force to be reckoned with economically and militarily. Sunni Ali Ber built the Songhay Empire in western Africa. Under Askia the Great's leadership, the Songhay Empire became the largest and wealthiest kingdom ever in western Africa. Afonso I spread Christianity in Kingdom of Kongo and brought wealth to the kingdom through trade with the Portuguese.

## PERFORMANCE OBJECTIVES

- To understand Elizabeth I's impact on religion and economics in England
- To explain the importance of Timbuktu as a center of Islamic study and trade
- To describe the effects of the slave trade on the Kingdom of Kongo

## BUILDING BACKGROUND

Ask students to define *leadership*. Invite them to list qualities that a good leader should possess and to cite examples of leaders who have demonstrated these qualities. Keep the list on display, and remind students to refer to it as they read. Tell them that they will read about four rulers whose leadership made their empires prominent and respected.

## CAST OF CHARACTERS

**Elizabeth I** Protestant queen of England

**Sunni Ali Ber** founder of the Songhay Empire

**Askia** (AKS-kee-ah) **"the Great" Muhamad** (moh-HAH-med) **Toure** (TOO-ray) ruler of Songhay Empire

**Afonso I** (ah-FAHN-soh) king of Kongo

## VOCABULARY

**monarch** someone who rules a nation or state, usually for life and by hereditary right

**negotiation** process of reaching agreements through discussions and compromise

**traditional** related to elements of a culture that are passed from generation to generation

**mosque** Muslim house of worship

**commerce** buying and selling of goods, especially between nations

## WORKING WITH PRIMARY SOURCES

Point out the quotations from Leo Africanus on pages 104 and 108. Discuss what the quotations reveal about the priorities of the rulers of Timbuktu. How would a focus on books and scholarship have affected the way in which the city and the kingdom were ruled? Invite students to learn more about Leo Africanus and Timbuktu at *http://en.wikipedia.org/wiki/Timbuktu*.

## GEOGRAPHY CONNECTION

**Location** Have students locate England on a map. Discuss the advantages and disadvantages that England may have had due to its location and its island geography.

## READING COMPREHENSION QUESTIONS

1. Why was Elizabeth Tudor imprisoned when she was a teenager? (*Her half-sister, the queen, believed that Elizabeth had supported a rebellion against her.*)
2. What assets did Elizabeth I have as a ruler? (*She was shrewd, could speak several languages, and used the possibility of marriage to negotiate with other leaders.*)
3. How did Elizabeth I win the support of both Catholics and Protestants during her reign? (*She allowed religious diversity as long as people were loyal to her.*)
4. In what ways did Sunni Ali Ber build the Songhay Empire? (*He conquered neighboring kingdoms, increased the size of his army, used a navy to patrol the Niger River, and helped his cities grow wealthy through trade.*)
5. What did Askia the Great do to support and spread Islam? (*He sought legal and political advice from Islamic scholars, supported the building of mosques, and encouraged the writing of books on Muslim history and law.*)

## CRITICAL THINKING QUESTIONS

1. Why was Elizabeth I's tolerance for religious diversity a key to stabilizing England's government? (*Disagreement about religion had been the source of conflict for many years. When religious differences were no longer a major issue, Elizabeth had more support from her people and could focus on strengthening the country's economy and using its military effectively.*)
2. Why do you think literature and the arts flourished during the Elizabethan Age? (*Writers and composers sought favor from Elizabeth. She enjoyed music and dancing and so she supported the work of composers. In a good economy, people are more able to take time for plays or concerts.*)
3. In what way did the arrival of Portuguese merchants bring about the decline of the Kingdom of Kongo? (*Merchants eventually made the slave trade a key part of their business. The slave trade decimated the Kongo population.*)

## SOCIAL SCIENCES

**Economics** The mix of economics and religion in Elizabethan England is still evident in the many "wool churches" found throughout the country. These churches were built with funds from merchants who became wealthy through England's wool trade. Have students use key words such as "wool church" to search the Internet for pictures of such churches and to investigate the areas of England that were prominent in the wool trade.

## READING AND LANGUAGE ARTS

**Reading Nonfiction** Have students compare and contrast the reigns of Elizabeth I, Sunni ali Ber, Askia the Great, and Afonso I. Students can use *Religion*, *Economy*, and *Military Strength* as headings on a three-column chart to note similarities and differences among the rulers.

**Using Language** The author uses vivid adjectives to describe Elizabeth I. Have students scan the chapter to make a list of the words used, and use the list to create a character sketch of the queen.

### THEN and NOW

Timbuktu was once a vibrant trading center as well as beacon for Islamic scholars. Today the city is impoverished, but it still attracts tourists who want to visit this legendary place.

### 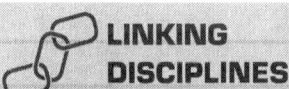 LINKING DISCIPLINES

**Science** In 1526, Afonso I asked the king of Portugal to send "good drugs and medicine" to help his people. At the time, the use of chemicals for healing was a new idea. Have students research the work of the alchemist Paracelsus, who pioneered the use of chemicals and minerals in healing illness and disease.

AN AGE OF VOYAGES, 1350–1600

## LITERATURE CONNECTION

There are numerous enjoyable books that will broaden students' knowledge of the empires of the powerful monarchs of England and Africa.

Forbath, Peter. *Lord of the Kongo: A Novel.* New York: Simon & Schuster, 1996. Historical Fiction. A 16th-century Portuguese cabin boy, stranded in the Congo, becomes involved with the prince who became King Afonso I. **ADVANCED**

Koslow, Philip. *Songhay: The Empire Builders.* New York: Chelsea House, 1995. Nonfiction. The leaders who built Africa's Songhay Empire are the focus of this book. **EASY**

Lasky, Kathryn. *Elizabeth I: Red Rose of the House of Tudor, England, 1544.* New York: Scholastic, 1999. Historical Fiction. A diary reveals the childhood of one the great monarchs of England. **AVERAGE**

## LITERACY TIPS

In addition to using the suggestions in the Supporting Learning and Extending Learning sections, refer back frequently to pages 16–19 for strategies and advice from a literacy coach.

## WRITING

**Journal Entry** Review Elizabeth I's speech to her troops at Tilbury on Student Edition page 101. Remind students that it was crucial that she assert her authority as a leader in her speech. Have students write a journal entry that Elizabeth might have written as she journeyed to meet the troops. What might she have been worried about, or excited about? How did she feel about the victory over the Spanish?

## SUPPORTING LEARNING

**English Language Learners** Point out that Elizabeth I used her knowledge of Latin to her advantage, and that many English words come from Latin. Suggest that students learn the meanings of Latin-based prefixes to help them understand words used in the chapter. Begin with common prefixes such as *inter-* in *international* or *de-* in *depopulate*. Have students list words using Latin prefixes in a personal dictionary.

**Struggling Readers** Guide students to create a two-column chart showing challenges and accomplishments of each ruler discussed in the chapter.

## EXTENDING LEARNING

**Enrichment** Invite students to learn more about the life of Elizabeth I's half sister Mary. Websites such as *http://tudorhistory.org/mary* or *http://en.wikipedia.org/wiki/Mary_I_of_England* may be helpful starting places for their research. Allow time for students to present their findings to the class.

**Extension** Have students write and present a conversation among the four rulers described in the chapter. Elizabeth I, Sunni ali Ber, Askia the Great, and Afonso I might discuss the challenges they faced as leaders, or the qualities that they believed were their strengths.

NAME _____ DATE _____

## AFRICAN STATES, 1550

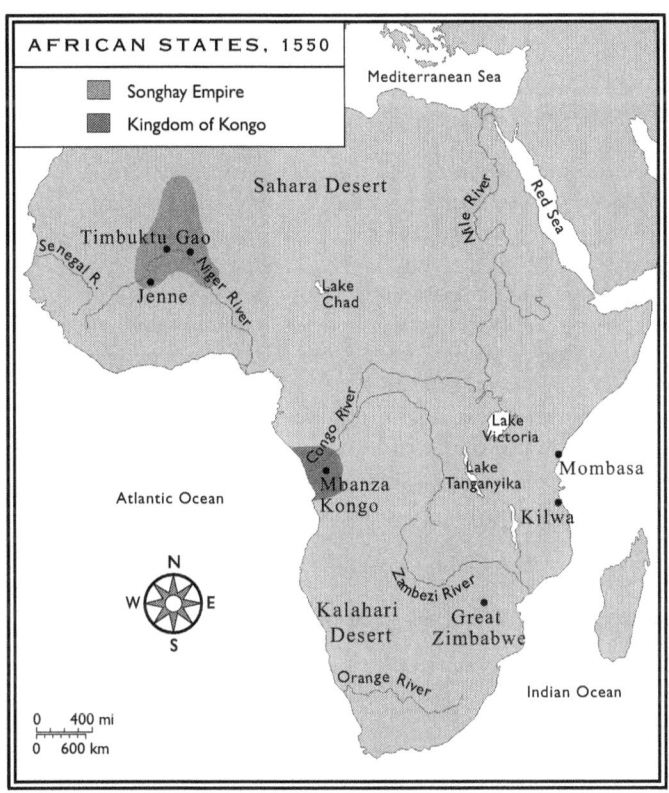

**Directions**

Use the map to answer the questions that follow.

1. What is similar about the geography of the Songhay Empire and the Kingdom of Kongo?
   _____

2. Use the scale of miles to describe the size of the Songhay Empire and the Kingdom of Kongo.
   _____
   _____

3. What made the cities of the Songhay Empire good meeting places for traders from the south and the east?
   _____
   _____

4. What geographic feature helped to protect the Songhay Empire from outside invaders?
   _____
   _____
   _____

5. What geographic features allowed the slave trade to flourish in the Kingdom of Kongo?
   _____
   _____
   _____

## THE HEART AND STOMACH OF A KING

**Directions**

This excerpt from Elizabeth I's speech to her troops at Tilbury, England also appears on Student Edition page 101. Read the speech, and answer the questions that follow.

> My loving people: we have been persuaded by some that are careful of our safety to take heed how we commit ourselves to armed multitudes for fear of treachery. But I assure you I do not desire to live to distrust my faithful and loving people. Let tyrants fear. I have always so behaved myself that, under God, I have placed my chiefest strength and safeguard in the loyal hearts and good will of my subjects. And therefore I am come amongst you, as you see, at this time, not for my recreation and disport, but being resolved in the midst and heat of battle to live or die amongst you all, to lay down for my God, and for my kingdom, and for my people, my honor and my blood, even in the dust. I know I have the body of a weak and feeble woman, but I have the heart and stomach of a king—and a king of England, too. I think foul scorn that Parma, or Spain, or any prince of Europe should dare to invade the borders of my realm. to which, rather than any dishonor shall grow by men, I myself will take up arms. I will be your general, judge, and rewarder.

1. Why do you think rulers used plural pronouns such as "we" to speak of themselves?

2. Why does Elizabeth believe that there is no need for her to be afraid to speak to her troops?

3. Why do you think Elizabeth promises "to live or die amongst" her troops?

4. What warning does Elizabeth give to any ruler who thinks England is vulnerable because its ruler is a woman?

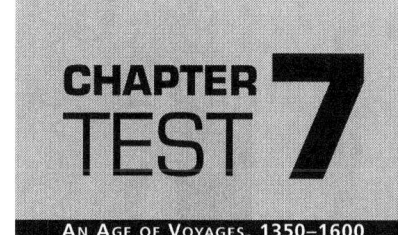

**NAME**            **DATE**

## A. MULTIPLE CHOICE

**Circle the letter of the best answer for each question.**

1. Which of the following was **not** an advantage for Queen Elizabeth I when she inherited her throne?
   a. the ability to speak several languages
   b. the stability of her country
   c. the fact that she was a woman
   d. her understanding of diplomacy

2. Which of the following describes Elizabeth I's policy regarding religion?
   a. All of her subjects were required to practice Islam.
   b. She allowed only Protestant religious practices.
   c. She allowed some religious diversity as long as people were loyal to her.
   d. She expected everyone in England to become Catholic.

3. Which city was a center for Islamic study and learning in the Songhay Empire?
   a. Mbanza      c. Gao
   b. Jenne        d. Timbuktu

4. What was the effect of the slave trade on the kingdom of the Kongo?
   a. The kingdom slowly broke apart.
   b. The kingdom flourished.
   c. The kingdom became a place to study Islam.
   d. The kingdom converted to Christianity.

## B. CAUSE AND EFFECT

**Complete the chart by writing an effect for each cause.**

| CAUSE | EFFECT |
|---|---|
| 5. Sunni Ali threatened to arrest Islamic scholars in Timbuktu. | |
| 6. Askia the Great decided that Islam could help unify his empire. | |
| 7. There were many similarities between Christian ideas and those of traditional African religions. | |

## C. SUPPORTING AN OPINION

On Student Edition page 100, the author states that Elizabeth "became one of the most effective monarchs England (or any country) ever had." Based on what you have read about her, do you agree with the author's statement? On a separate sheet of paper, write a paragraph explaining your answer. Use details from the chapter to support your opinion.

# CHAPTER 8

# "EVERYTHING THE WORLD HAS TO OFFER": CITY LIFE  PAGES 109–121

**FOR HOMEWORK**

Student Study Guide pages 39–42

**CAST OF CHARACTERS**

**Cortés** (kohr-TEHZ), **Hernán** (ehr-NAHN) Spanish explorer and conqueror of the Aztec Empire

**Moctezuma** (mok-te-ZOO-mah) II Aztec emperor

## CHAPTER SUMMARY

City life in the 15th through mid-17th centuries offered people varied opportunities for work, leisure, and worship but also had many dangers. Trade was an important part of a city's economy, and goods and people came to cities from many places. Many of the world's largest cities were capitals, and some had hundreds of thousands of residents. Diseases and fire spread quickly and easily in crowded cities. Crime, filth, and poverty were other problems.

## PERFORMANCE OBJECTIVES

- To understand the opportunities and problems of city life in the 15th through mid-17th centuries
- To describe the roles of people in cities, including class structures, family life, warfare, religious beliefs and practices, and slavery
- To explain the importance of Florence in the early stages of the Renaissance and the growth of independent trading cities, such as Venice

## BUILDING BACKGROUND

Ask students to share what they know about the benefits and drawbacks of living in modern cities. Then ask them to predict what city life was like in the 1400s through mid-1600s. List their answers in a chart. As students read the chapter, have them note how city life in the 15th through mid-17th centuries compares to city life today.

## VOCABULARY

**capital** a city that is the seat of government

**bureaucrats** administrators of a government or other organization

**bishops** high-ranking religious leaders in Christian churches

**prophecy** prediction

**immigrants** people who leave one country or area and settle in another place

**council** people who are elected or appointed to make laws, policies, or decisions

**servants** people who work for wages in other people's households

**slaves** people who are forced to work for others

## WORKING WITH PRIMARY SOURCES

Direct students to the quotation from Ludovico Guicciardini on Student Edition page 110. Ask them to identify the point of view from which Guicciardini writes about Antwerp and to explain how this may influence his point of view of the city and its inhabitants.

**68** CHAPTER 8

## GEOGRAPHY CONNECTION

**Location and Region** Ask students what the map on page 112 shows. Then ask students to write a description of the regions in which most of the major cities on the map are located. Use the activity to assess students' understanding of the geographic factors that influence a city's growth.

## READING COMPREHENSION QUESTIONS

1. What sorts of jobs did people have in cities in the 1500s and 1600s? (*People could work as shopkeepers, craftsmen, servants; some might work as government officials, bureaucrats, or lawyers.*)

2. What can people learn by studying historical documents, such as diaries and letters, of travelers to cities in the 15th and 16th centuries? (*People can discover what city life was like at the time the travelers wrote the documents.*)

3. Why were capital cities filled with officials, nobles, lawyers, and bureaucrats? (*These people hoped to gain power and influence through their dealings with the ruler.*)

4. What might happen to children who were caught begging in cities? (*They might be sold into slavery. In European cities, they might be transported to the new colonies to work as indentured servants.*)

5. Why did European cities smell worse than the Aztec capital of Tenochtitlan? (*In European cities, people threw trash into the streets, animal droppings stayed where they fell, and latrines and outhouses filled up and overflowed. In Tenochtitlan, human and animal waste and most kinds of garbage were taken away from the city by canoe.*)

## CRITICAL THINKING QUESTIONS

1. Why did many immigrants move to cities? (*Cities offered opportunities that could lead to a better, or at least a different, life. Also, during times of famine and war, many poor people moved to cities to seek support from churches or charitable groups.*)

2. What do you think contributed to the wealth and importance of cities such as Florence and Venice? (*trade*)

3. What facts support the generalization that worship was an important activity in cities? (*Visitors to cities, including Rome, Istanbul, Ahmedabad, and Tenochtitlan, commented on the cities' religious buildings, some of which were crowded with worshippers, altars, and artwork. Tenochtitlan had a huge religious center with many temples.*)

## SOCIAL SCIENCES

**Economics** Have partners make two lists in their history journals: one of the occupations that city dwellers had in the 15th and 16th centuries and one of occupations that city dwellers have today. Have students compare the lists and explain why some jobs still exist today and others are different.

### THEN and NOW

Executions were public events in London in the 1600s, but today capital punishment does not exist in Great Britain. England banned public executions in 1868 and abolished capital punishment in 1965.

### LINKING DISCIPLINES

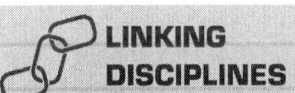

**Art** Invite students to use encyclopedias and online resources to learn more about the architecture of the Forbidden City, the temple complexes at Tenochtitlan, or the Tower of London. Students can make a labeled diagram of the structure to share their findings.

AN AGE OF VOYAGES, 1350–1600

## LITERATURE CONNECTION

There are numerous enjoyable books that will broaden students' knowledge of city life during the Renaissance.

Bessire, Mark. *Great Zimbabwe*. London: Franklin Watts, 1999. Nonfiction. This book examines the history and culture of this prominent trading city. EASY

Hinds, Kathryn. *The City*. New York: Benchmark Books, 2003. Nonfiction. Everything from cultural life to health issues is discussed in this description of life in medieval cities. EASY

Hooper, Mary. *Petals in the Ashes*. New York: Bloomsbury USA Children's Books, 2004. Historical Fiction. Two young girls face life in London in the aftermath of the Great Fire. AVERAGE

## LITERACY TIPS

In addition to using the suggestions in the Supporting Learning and Extending Learning sections, refer back frequently to pages 16–19 for strategies and advice from a literacy coach.

## READING AND LANGUAGE ARTS

**Reading Nonfiction** Ask students to look closely at each image in Chapter 8 and explain the information it gives. Work with students to relate each image to an aspect of city life that is described in the chapter.

## WRITING

**Description** Invite students to write a description of one of the cities they read about in Chapter 8. Before students write, tell them to take notes about the city's appearance and to refer to their notes to make an outline. Tell students to use exact nouns, figurative language, and details to describe what the city looked like in the 16th or early 17th century. You many wish to create a class book of the city descriptions for the classroom library.

**Using Language** Direct attention to the word *thieves* and *robbers* in the fourth sentence on page 109. Point out that the use of the exact nouns makes the sentence clearer and more vivid than it would be if Waldstein used the generic word *people*. Have students identify other exact nouns in the chapter and generic words that could replace them. Ask students which words make the writing clearer and why.

## SUPPORTING LEARNING

**English Language Learners** Work with students to create lists of words that fit into categories such as leisure, work, and worship. Use visuals and pantomime to help students understand word meanings. Then guide students in using the words to summarize what people in cities did in the 15th and 16th centuries.

**Struggling Readers** Before students read the chapter, conduct a chapter walk with them. As students read, have them list the positives and negatives of city life in a two-column chart titled *City Life in the 1400s–Mid-1600s*.

## EXTENDING LEARNING

**Enrichment** Invite students to use encyclopedias and other nonfiction resources to investigate the class structures in cities such as Tenochtitlan, London, Paris, and Beijing during the 15th and 16th centuries. Students can share their findings by preparing a chart that compares and contrasts the class structures of the cities.

**Extension** Have students work in groups to create a diagram or model of a city that incorporates features from several of the cities they studied in Chapter 8. Invite students to present their models to the class and to identify the sources of the borrowed features.

# MAJOR CITIES OF THE WORLD, 1500

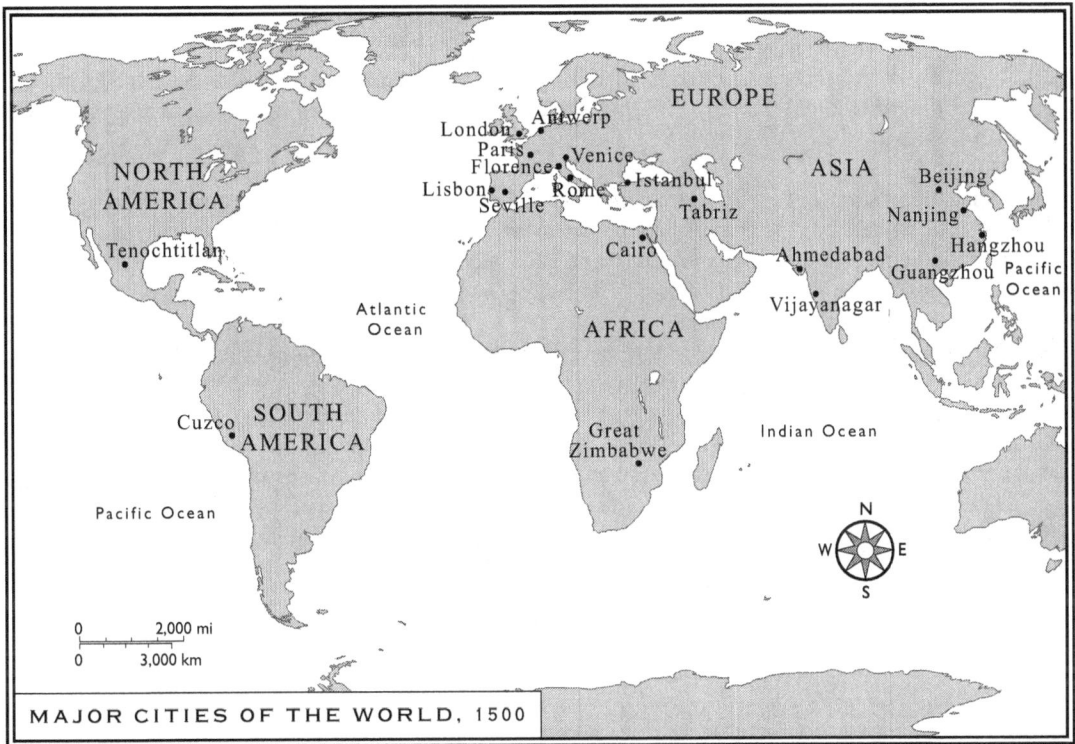

MAJOR CITIES OF THE WORLD, 1500

**Directions**
Use the map to answer the questions that follow.

1. On what continent were the cities of Ahmedabad and Beijing located?
   _____

2. What body of water separated Ahmedabad from Great Zimbabwe?
   _____
   _____

3. Describe the most direct route for travelers from Lisbon to Tenochtitlan.
   _____
   _____

4. Which two cities are nearest each other?
   _____

5. Use the scale of miles to find the distance between the following cities.
   Venice and Paris _____
   Beijing and Antwerp _____
   London and Tenochtitlan _____

## GOOD HOUSES AND PLEASANT GARDENS

**Directions**

This excerpt from the Hernán Cortés's letter to King Charles V of Spain also appears on Student Edition page 115. In it, he describes the Aztec city of Tenochtitlan. Read the letter and, with a partner, answer the questions that follow.

> This city has many squares where trading is done and markets are held continuously. There is also one square twice as big as that of Salamanca, with arcades all around, where more than sixty thousand people come each day to buy and sell, and where every kind of merchandise produced in these lands is found: provisions as well as ornaments of gold and silver, lead, brass, copper, tin, stones, shells, bones, and feathers. . . . There is in this great square a very large building like a courthouse, where ten or twelve persons sit as judges. They preside over all that happens in the markets, and sentence criminals.
>
> There are, in all districts of this great city, many temples. . . . There are in the city many large and beautiful houses, and the reason for this is that all the chiefs in the lands, who are Moctezuma's vassals [men who owe allegiance to Moctezuma], have houses in the city and live there for part of the year; and in addition there are many rich citizens who likewise have very good houses. All of these houses have very large and very good rooms and also very pleasant gardens of various sorts of flowers both on the upper and lower floors.

1. What were Cortés's feelings about Tenochtitlan? Explain.

2. What details does Cortés include to support the main idea statement "This city has many squares where trading is done and markets are held continuously"?

3. What fact that Cortés includes would support the following generalization: Religion was important to the Aztecs?

4. What generalization can you make about Moctezuma's vassals?

**NAME**            **DATE**

## A. MULTIPLE CHOICE

**Circle the letter of the best answer for each question.**

1. Which of the following was not a type of work in cities in 1600?
   - **a.** listening to music
   - **b.** cooking
   - **c.** waitressing
   - **d.** goldsmithing

2. What surrounded the Forbidden City?
   - **a.** a ring of temples
   - **b.** a palace complex
   - **c.** rings of walls
   - **d.** cannons

3. Which of the following especially supported the growth of cities in 1600?
   - **a.** farming
   - **b.** trade
   - **c.** military strength
   - **d.** religion

4. Why were there more deaths than births in cities?
   - **a.** Cities had many fires.
   - **b.** The streets were too busy.
   - **c.** Diseases spread easily in crowded conditions.
   - **d.** Healthful food was not available in cities.

## B. SHORT ANSWER

**Respond to each question in two or three sentences.**

5. Describe three opportunities people found in cities.
   _____
   _____
   _____

6. Describe three problems people faced in cities.
   _____
   _____
   _____

## C. ANALYZING A GENERALIZATION

On Student Edition page 111, the author states, "Visitors to any city would find shopkeepers and public markets selling imported luxuries and locally produced goods." Do you agree with the author's generalization? On a separate sheet of paper, write an essay explaining your answer. Use facts from the chapter to support your answer.

# CHAPTER 9

# SILK AND SPICES: TRAVEL AND TRADE IN THE MEDITERRANEAN SEA AND THE INDIAN OCEAN PAGES 122–135

**FOR HOMEWORK**

Student Study Guide pages 43–46

**CAST OF CHARACTERS**

**Zheng** (jehng) **He** (heh) Chinese admiral who headed naval expeditions to the Indian Ocean

**Henry "the Navigator"** prince of Portugal who supported voyages of exploration and trade

**Dias** (DEE-as), **Bartolomeu** (bahr-TAHL-oh-mew) Portuguese captain who rounded the southern tip of Africa

**Da Gama** (duh GAH-muh), **Vasco** (VAHSH-koh) Portuguese captain who first reached India by sailing around Africa

## CHAPTER SUMMARY

Early in the 15th century, the Chinese admiral Zheng He made several voyages across the Indian Ocean and the South China Sea, bringing Chinese silk, porcelain, and other luxury goods to trade with foreign rulers. By the time of the European Renaissance, trade routes extended to the Mediterranean Sea and were highly profitable for European traders. The Portuguese, supported by Prince Henry the Navigator, were the early leaders in voyages of commerce and discovery.

## PERFORMANCE OBJECTIVES

▶ To understand what motivated early international trade
▶ To describe what goods were sought after by European merchants
▶ To compare and contrast overland and sea trading routes
▶ To understand how Islam influenced and encouraged trade
▶ To describe the early leadership of Portugal in exploration and trade

## BUILDING BACKGROUND

Ask students to share their knowledge about trading. If necessary, point out that some students may trade as part of hobbies such as collecting baseball cards or stamps. Lead students to understand that each side of a trade must have something that the other side wants. Tell them that they will read about early trading that linked Europe with Asian nations.

## VOCABULARY

**emperor** the ruler of an empire

**fleet** a group of ships sailing together, under the command of one admiral

**cargo** the goods carried by a ship; freight

**admiral** the commanding officer of a navy or fleet

**merchant** a person who buys and sells goods for profit; a trader

**luxury goods** products that are not necessary for basic survival

**cosmopolitan** representing many different cultures

**astronomical charts** maplike graphics showing the positions of stars and constellations, used by sea captains to estimate position and gauge direction

As needed, have students consult the glossary to define the following word: *sakk*.

## WORKING WITH PRIMARY SOURCES

Point out the sidebar on Student Edition page 132 and remind students that Marco Polo is known for his reports on his travels to China. Discuss his observations about trade in Madagascar, and have volunteers explain the difference between *trade* and *barter*.

## GEOGRAPHY CONNECTION

**Interaction** Direct attention to the map on Student Edition page 129, and discuss the geographic factors that affected interactions among Asia, Africa, and Europe in the 15th century. Point out the strip of land that separates the Red Sea from the Mediterranean Sea and explain that until the Suez Canal was dug late in the 19th century, ships had to circumnavigate Africa to travel from Europe to Asia.

## READING COMPREHENSION QUESTIONS

1. Why were the ships in Zheng He's fleet designed to be so huge and impressive? *(They were designed to impress the people they visited, to reflect the power of the Chinese emperor, and to persuade the people to submit.)*

2. Why did it prove impossible for Chinese and Byzantine emperors to control the spread of silk-making technology? *(People easily stole silkworms and mulberry seeds.)*

3. What was the major reason that merchants were eager to trade with India, China, and the Spice Islands? *(They hoped to become wealthy by obtaining and reselling such luxury goods as silk and spices.)*

4. Why could only the wealthiest people afford most of the goods brought back from Asia? *(They were luxury goods to begin with—silk, pearls, jewels, spices—and merchants tacked on transport and handling costs.)*

5. Give some examples of spices that Europeans were able to obtain in the Spice Islands. What were their uses? *(Examples include pepper, cloves, nutmeg, mace, cardamom, cinnamon, and ginger. They were used to flavor food; to preserve meats and to disguise the taste of spoiled meat; to scent perfumes and love potions; and as painkillers.)*

## CRITICAL THINKING QUESTIONS

1. Why were the sea routes important for trade? *(Land routes were hard to maintain and could be dangerous. Carrying goods by camel or wagon was very expensive. It was cheaper and easier to load everything onto ships.)*

2. How did the spread of Islam encourage trade? *(Islamic law covered many aspects of business, such as contracts. Therefore, merchants could be confident in the uniformity of laws governing trade in different Islam societies.)*

3. Why did trade bring cultural diversity to port cities in the 15th century? *(People of different cultures and religions came to port cities, all intent on trading with foreigners and gaining wealth. Different customs and languages mixed in the marketplace.)*

## SOCIAL SCIENCES

**Economics** Remind students that Chinese officials decided that Zheng He's voyages were too expensive to continue, while European monarchs decided to support exploration and trade. Invite students to conduct a cost-benefit analysis for both societies. Ask them to review the chapter to identify factors, such as the costs of war against the Mongols, that influenced the decisions in each society.

### THEN and NOW

In 1497, it took Vasco da Gama more than nine months to sail from Portugal to the western coast of India. Modern travelers fly nonstop from Lisbon to Bombay in less than twelve hours.

### 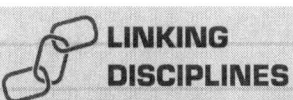 LINKING DISCIPLINES

**Mathematics** Challenge students to develop word problems based on information presented in the chapter. For example, based on the information presented on Student Edition page 122, students might write word problems about the perimeter and area of the largest of Zheng He's ships.

AN AGE OF VOYAGES, 1350–1600

**LITERATURE CONNECTION**

There are numerous enjoyable books that will broaden students' knowledge of trade and travel in the medieval world.

Franck, Irene and David M. Brownstone. *Across Asia by Land.* New York: Facts on File, 1991. Nonfiction. The authors survey the history of trade routes in Asia. ADVANCED

Ross, Val. *The Road to There: Mapmakers and Their Stories.* Toronto: Tundra Books, 2003. Nonfiction. The stories of assorted mapmakers reveal a different aspect of trade and exploration. EASY

**LITERACY TIPS**

In addition to using the suggestions in the Supporting Learning and Extending Learning sections, refer back frequently to pages 16–19 for strategies and advice from a literacy coach.

## READING AND LANGUAGE ARTS

**Reading Nonfiction** Have students develop a ten-question chapter quiz, along with a separate answer key. Remind students that quiz questions should deal with the most important points in the chapter. Have students exchange quizzes with a partner, and then correct each other's answers. Use the activity to assess students' understanding of chapter content.

**Using Language** Review Student Edition pages 133–134 and discuss how such precise verbs as *inched, cut, press,* and *rounded* help readers to understand the movements and speeds of the merchant ships. Invite students to create a list of other examples of precise language in the chapter.

## WRITING

**Ship's Log** Have students imagine that they are captains in either Zheng He's or Vasco da Gama's fleets. Direct them to use details from the text, as well as details about imaginary characters, to write a fictional ship's log covering three or four days at sea.

## SUPPORTING LEARNING

**English Language Learners** Gather products such as silk, cinnamon sticks, nutmeg, pepper, and silver, and work with students to name and describe each one. Distribute samples of one commodity to each student "merchant," who becomes a silk trader or a cinnamon trader. Then have students act out a scene in a marketplace, offering what each of them has in return for something else that they want.

**Struggling Readers** Brainstorm a list of things a merchant would have to do before, during, and after trading, such as acquire a product to sell, prepare for a trade journey, and return home with new products for trade. Have students use the sequence of events chart at the back of the book to put events in a logical sequence.

## EXTENDING LEARNING

**Enrichment** Have students research modern trade between the nations of Europe and such trading partners as China, India, and Indonesia. What products are traded? You may wish to have students identify countries to investigate at *www.infoplease.com/countries.html*. Allow time for volunteers to share their findings with the class orally.

**Extension** Suggest that in a port city with many merchants it must have been important to appeal to buyers. Have students work with partners or in small groups to create posters and other materials that a merchant could use to advertise and display products such as silk or spices.

## EURASIAN EXPLORATION AND TRADE, 1405-1500

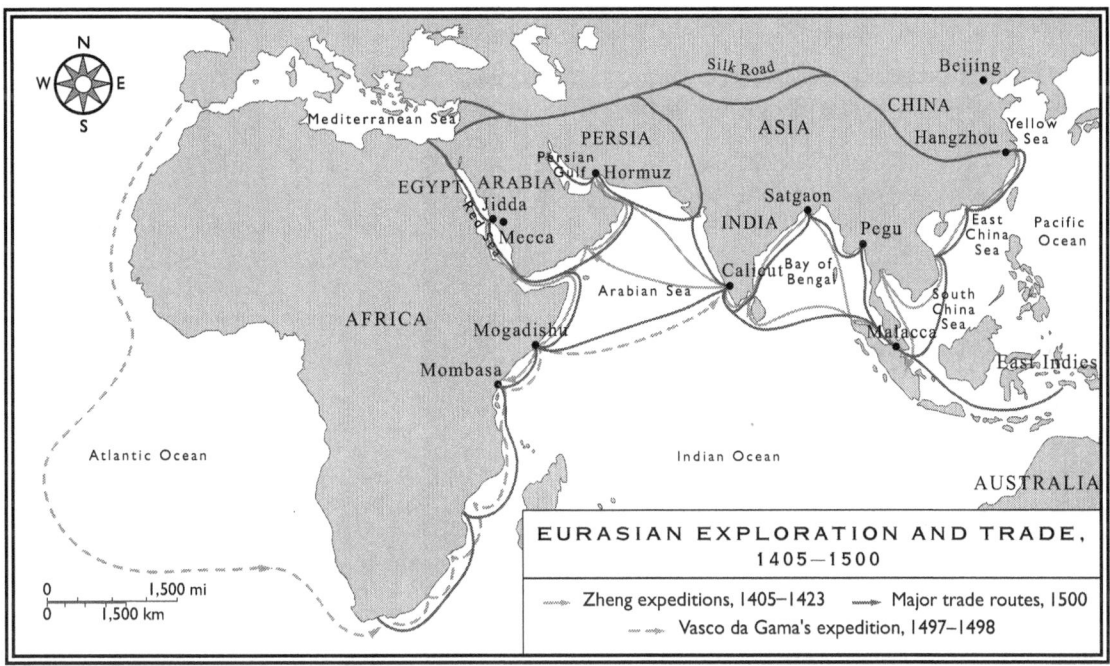

**Directions**

Use the map to answer the questions that follow.

1. What is similar about the routes of Zheng He's expeditions and the major trade routes of 1500?

2. Use the scale of miles to tell the approximate length of the northern Silk Road, from the Mediterranean Sea to Hangzhou, China.

3. What city in India was a major trading port?

4. What combination of land and sea routes would merchants take to get from the Mediterranean Sea to Mogadishu, on the west coast of Africa?

5. If a merchant wanted to sail from Calicut to Hormuz, about how many miles long is the most direct route?

## THE PEOPLE ARE ALL RICH

**Directions**

Entries from Ma Huan's journals appear on Student Edition page 124. Read the following excerpts. Then answer the questions that follow with a partner.

**EXCERPT A**
[On the port city of Hormuz in the Persian Gulf]
Setting sail . . . you go towards the north-west; and you reach this place after sailing with a fair wind for twenty-five days. The capital lies behind the sea and up against the mountains.

Foreign ships from every place and foreign merchants traveling by land all come to this country to attend the market and trade; hence the people are all rich. . . .

**EXCERPT B**
[On western India]
As to the pepper: the inhabitants of the mountainous countryside have established gardens, and it is extensively cultivated. When the period of the tenth moon arrives, the pepper ripens; [and] it is collected, dried in the sun, and sold. . . . if there is a buyer, an official gives permission for the sale; the duty [that is, the sales tax] is calculated according to the amount of the purchase price and is paid in to the authorities. Each one po-ho [a measure of weight] is sold for two hundred gold coins.

1. How might the information in Excerpt A have been useful to merchants planning a trip to Hormuz?

2. Do you think the information in Excerpt A would encourage or discourage merchants regarding the trip? Explain.

3. How might the information in Excerpt B have been useful to merchants interested in buying pepper?

4. Based on the information in Excerpt B, do you think government officials encouraged the farmers to grow a lot of pepper? Explain.

**NAME**            **DATE**

## A. MULTIPLE CHOICE

**Circle the letter of the best answer to each question.**

1. The Chinese rulers judged Zheng He's voyages to be unsuccessful because
    a. he failed to get any foreign rulers to submit to the Chinese emperor.
    b. his huge ships eventually rotted away.
    c. he failed to find a sea route to the east coast of Africa.
    d. his voyages cost more money than they brought in.

2. By 1500, cities like Venice became busy and profitable centers because
    a. Chinese rulers no longer pursued naval interests.
    b. they were trading ports, where many people came to buy and sell goods.
    c. the doge held annual harbor festivals.
    d. they developed a European silk industry that produced affordable silk fabrics.

3. Vasco da Gama proved to be more successful than Bartolomeu Dias because
    a. he found a sea route to connect Portugal with India.
    b. he was the first to sail around the southern tip of Africa.
    c. he founded a Portuguese colony on the island of Madeira.
    d. his voyages led him to design and develop the astrolabe.

4. Most of the goods traded over the land routes were very expensive because
    a. people used the stones from the road for building and repairing houses.
    b. land routes were dusty and often dangerous roads.
    c. they were handmade by highly skilled artists and craftspeople.
    d. merchants added transport and handling charges to the price.

## B. SHORT ANSWER

**Write one or two sentences to answer each question.**

5. Two important luxury goods were traded along the silk roads. One was silk. Describe the other product and tell why it was important. _____

_____

6. How did the spread of Islam encourage international trade? _____

_____

7. Why was Prince Henry of Portugal known as "Henry the Navigator"? _____

_____

## C. ESSAY

**On the lines below, write a short essay explaining how the compass, astrolabe, and astronomical charts helped early sea captains.** _____

_____

_____

_____

_____

_____

# CHAPTER 10

## "COLUMBIA" OR "AMERICA"? NAMES AND FAME IN A "NEW WORLD"
### PAGES 136–151

**Student Study Guide pages 47–50**

### CAST OF CHARACTERS

**Columbus, Christopher** Italian explorer, first European since the Vikings to cross the Atlantic

**Cabot, John** (born Giovanni Caboto) Genoese sea captain who headed the first English expedition to North America

**Vespucci** (veh-SPOO-chee), **Amerigo** (ah-MEHR-ee-goh) Italian entrepreneur and explorer whose name was given to the Americas

**Cabral** (kuh-BRAHL), **Pedro Alvares** (AHL-vuh-res) Portuguese adventurer who first landed in what is now Brazil

## CHAPTER SUMMARY

Evidence shows that in about 1000 the Vikings became the first Europeans to cross the Atlantic to what is now Canada. In 1492, Christopher Columbus got the support of Queen Isabella of Spain to sail west to obtain Asian goods. News of Columbus's voyages prompted other expeditions. These voyages led to exchanges of crops and culture but also resulted in disease and death.

## PERFORMANCE OBJECTIVES

▶ To analyze the impact of voyages of discovery and the locations of the routes
▶ To know the influence of cartography in the development of a new European worldview
▶ To describe the exchange of plants, animals, technology, culture, and ideas among societies on different continents

## BUILDING BACKGROUND

Ask students to share what they have been taught about Christopher Columbus, and list their ideas on the chalkboard. Then read aloud the last two sentences of the first paragraph on Student Edition page 136, beginning with "Did his voyages lead . . ." Explain that as they read about Columbus and other explorers in this chapter, they should evaluate the facts to form their own opinions.

## VOCABULARY

**colony** an area of land ruled by a foreign government

**saga** a story about brave deeds, often passed down through generations

**mariner** one who operates or who helps operate a ship

**caravel** ship carrying several different types of sails to aid movement

**lateen sail** a triangular-shaped sail that allows a ship to travel into the wind

**astrolabe** a medieval instrument used to find the position of the sun or the stars

## WORKING WITH PRIMARY SOURCES

Read aloud the sidebar on Student Edition page 145, including the description of the source of the text. Ask students why the author points out that the proclamation was delivered in Spanish. Discuss how the Spanish Inquisition may relate to this proclamation. Tell students that they can read more about the Spanish Inquisition at *www.bartleby.com/65/in/Inquisit.html*.

## GEOGRAPHY CONNECTION

**Movement** Have students trace a route on a map from Iceland to Greenland to Newfoundland, Canada. Have them draw conclusions about the Vikings' challenging traveling conditions based on the route and their prior knowledge. You may also wish to have students investigate and report on the impact that ocean currents may have had on voyages to North America.

## READING COMPREHENSION QUESTIONS

1. What sources did Christopher Columbus use to predict that the world was round? *(the practical experience of sailors and books on geography and astronomy written by ancient Greeks and Egyptians)*
2. Why was Greenland described as "the first real-estate scam"? *(It was called "Greenland" to attract settlers from Norway, but there was little green land and few trees.)*
3. What was the economic reason for Christopher Columbus's voyages west? *(He wanted to obtain Asian silks and spices.)*
4. What was the purpose of the pope's Line of Demarcation? *(to divide the world into Spanish and Portuguese zones)*
5. What were some of the difficulties that Magellan and his expedition encountered? *(terrible weather; one ship sank; one ship mutinied; they ran out of food and suffered from scurvy; they burned some houses in the Philippines and were attacked in return; only one ship with 18 survivors made it back to Spain)*

## CRITICAL THINKING QUESTIONS

1. How have interpretations of Columbus's voyages changed over time? Give an example. *(Possible answer: People today might see positive aspects, such as the global exchanges of crops, and negative aspects, such as the spread of deadly diseases.)*
2. How did the events in Granada in 1492 affect Christopher Columbus's plans? *(The Spanish monarchs had defeated the Muslims, and they wanted to continue spreading Christianity and keep Spanish soldiers busy. As a result of good timing, Columbus received help from Queen Isabella.)*
3. How did the error in Columbus's plans affect the native people he encountered? *(Columbus misunderstood geography and thought he had landed in the Indies. Because of Columbus's error, he looked for gold and other riches he expected in the Indies, and he enslaved native peoples to help him find it.)*
4. Why do you think the Line of Demarcation had little effect on future expeditions and settlements? *(The pope ignored other European countries in favor of two Catholic countries, Portugal and Spain.)*

## SOCIAL SCIENCES

**Science, Technology, and Society** Suggest that students research one of the navigational tools used by early explorers, such as the astrolabe or the compass. Have them make an annotated diagram to explain how it worked to present their findings to the class. A useful website is *www.nps.gov/fora/navigation.htm*.

## READING AND LANGUAGE ARTS

**Reading Nonfiction** Have students compare and contrast the voyages of the explorers discussed in the chapter. Students can use *Dates, Routes, Financial Backers,* and *Results* as headings on a four-column chart to note similarities and differences among the explorers. Use the activity to assess students' understanding of chapter content.

**Using Language** Direct students to the phrase "Greenland itself is often described as the first real-estate scam." Point out that *scam* is a slang term that means "fraudulent business scheme," and that using slang adds immediacy to the language. Have students think of other slang terms to describe the Viking explorations. Other examples of slang may be found at *www.manythings.org/slang*.

AN AGE OF VOYAGES, 1350–1600

---

### THEN and NOW

Archaeologists continue to excavate sites associated with the Vikings in Newfoundland, Canada. They have found evidence of trade between the Vikings and native peoples, including an oval soapstone lamp most likely carved by a Dorset Eskimo from northern Canada. Dorset Eskimo, now called Inuit, still make beautiful carvings of soapstone that are sold around the world, often for thousands of dollars.

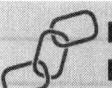

### LINKING DISCIPLINES

**Mathematics** Have students use a map and its scale to determine the distance between the Canary Islands and Japan. Have them use that amount and the incorrect distance Christopher Columbus used—2,500 miles—to determine Columbus's error. Tell them to show the error as a percent.

## LITERATURE CONNECTION

There are numerous enjoyable books that will broaden students' knowledge of the impact of Columbus's arrival in the Americas.

Dorris, Michael. *Morning Girl*. Santillana, Spain: Alfaguara Ediciones, SA, 1996. Historical Fiction. A Taino brother and sister describe their lives before and after the arrival of Christopher Columbus. EASY

O'Connor, Genevieve. *The Admiral and the Deck Boy: One Boy's Journey with Christopher Columbus*. White Hall, VA: Shoe Tree Press, 1991. Historical Fiction. A boy learns about life at sea at the side of Christopher Columbus as they sail to the "New World." AVERAGE

Torrey, Michele. *To the Edge of the World*. New York: Knopf Books for Young Readers, 2003. Historical Fiction. The journey of Ferdinand Magellan provides far more than a desperately-needed job for 14-year-old Mateo. AVERAGE

## LITERACY TIPS

In addition to using the suggestions in the Supporting Learning and Extending Learning sections, refer back frequently to pages 16–19 for strategies and advice from a literacy coach.

## WRITING

**Write a Persuasive Speech** Have students imagine that they are an explorer looking for backing for an expedition. Tell them to use details from the chapter to write a persuasive speech to a monarch, asking for funding and describing the economic benefits.

## SUPPORTING LEARNING

**English Language Learners** Work with students to list places in the chapter that were named by explorers. Have them point to each location on a map. Help students associate the places with the explorers who named them, such as Greenland with Erik the Red. Categorize names that come from other languages, such as San Salvador or Brazil, and those that are compounds such as Newfoundland.

**Struggling Readers** As students read, have them pause periodically to look for sequence words, place names, and distances to help them track the progress of the expeditions in their minds.

## EXTENDING LEARNING

**Enrichment** Have students use media center or Internet resources to find out about one of the native cultures encountered by Columbus or another explorer. For instance, they can research the Taino at *www.elboricua.com/history.html*. Remind them to frame questions to narrow their research.

**Extension** Invite pairs of students to make a historical map of Magellan's journey around the world. Direct them to prepare an oral presentation to accompany their maps.

**NAME** _____ **DATE** _____

## COLUMBUS'S VOYAGES, 1492–1502

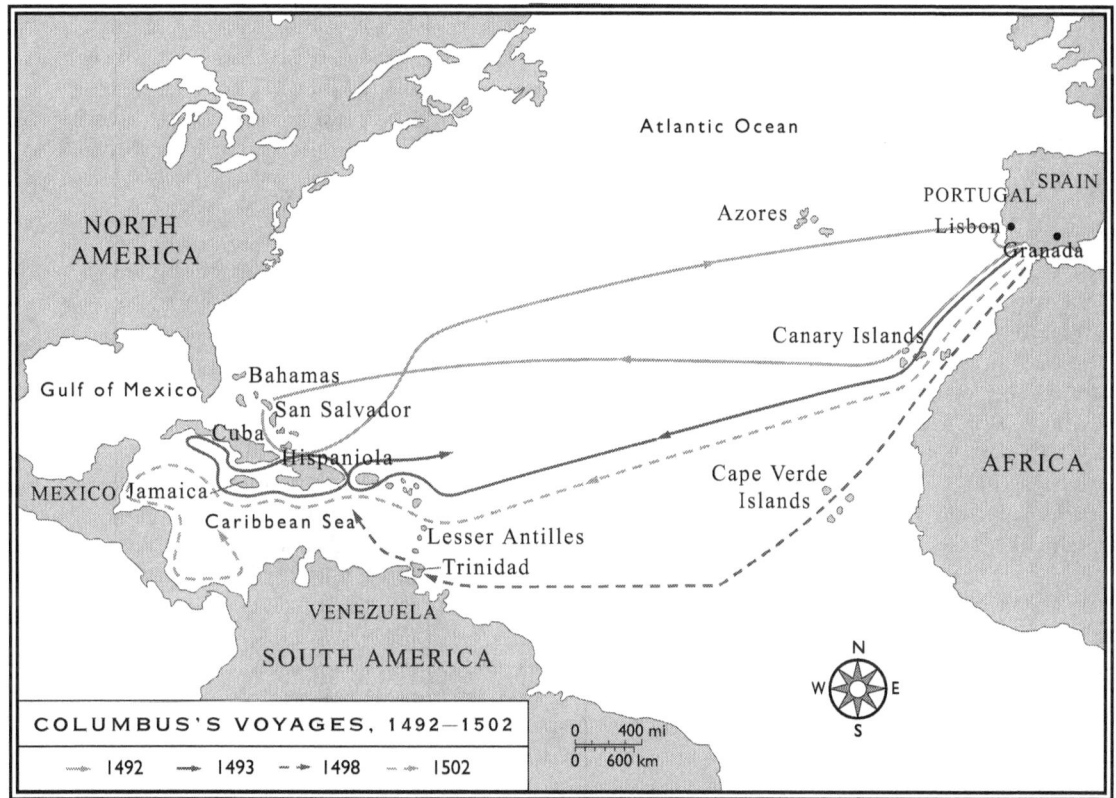

**Directions**

Use the map to answer the questions that follow.

**1.** In which year did Columbus explore the coast of what is now Mexico?
_____

**2.** Why do you think Columbus chose a route that passed by the Canary Islands?
_____

**3.** What is the approximate distance of Columbus's route in 1492 between the Canary Islands and San Salvador? _____

**4.** If it took Columbus approximately 5 weeks to sail from the Canary Islands to San Salvador, about how many miles did he sail per day? _____

**5.** When did Columbus explore what is now Venezuela? Based on what you read, why was the exploration important? _____
_____
_____
_____

CHAPTER 10 BLM      AN AGE OF VOYAGES, 1350–1600

AN AGE OF VOYAGES, 1350–1600      **NAME**                    **DATE**

## WISH YOU WERE HERE

**Directions**

The following text is from *The Medieval & Early Modern World Primary Sources and Reference Volume*, pages 72–74. It is an excerpt from a letter Christopher Columbus wrote to Queen Isabella in 1492. He wrote about his encounters with the native people of Hispana, in what is now Haiti. Read the excerpt with a partner, and answer the questions that follow. If necessary, check a dictionary for help with unfamiliar words.

> [The inhabitants of Hispana] are all, as I said before, unprovided with any sort of iron, and they are destitute of arms, which are entirely unknown to them, and for which they are not adapted; not on account of any bodily deformity, for they are well-made, but because they are timid and full of terror. . . . They are very guileless and honest, and very liberal of all they have. No one refuses the asker anything that he possesses; on the contrary, they themselves invite us to ask for it. They manifest affection toward all of us, exchanging valuable things for trifles, content with the very least thing or nothing at all.
>
> They do not practise idolatry; on the contrary, they believe that all strength, all power, in short, all blessings, are from Heaven, and that I have come down from there with these ships and sailors; and in this spirit was I received everywhere, after they had got over their fear. They are neither lazy nor awkward, but, on the contrary, are of an excellent and acute understanding. Those who have sailed these seas give excellent accounts of everything; but they have never seen men wearing clothes, or ships like ours.

**1.** What does Columbus mean by "they are destitute of arms"?

_____
_____
_____
_____

**2.** Look up the word *guileless*. Why do you think Columbus chose that word to describe the people of Hispana?

_____
_____
_____
_____

**3.** In what ways did Columbus respect the people he encountered? In what ways did he not show respect?

_____
_____
_____
_____

**4.** How might other Europeans have viewed the Spanish expedition?

_____
_____
_____
_____

# CHAPTER TEST 10

**AN AGE OF VOYAGES, 1350–1600**

## A. MULTIPLE CHOICE

**Circle the letter of the best answer for each question.**

1. Which explorer made the first English voyage to North America?
   a. Pedro Alvares Cabral
   b. Amerigo Vespucci
   c. John Cabot
   d. Erik the Red

2. Which of the following was **not** a reason for Columbus's first expedition?
   a. to claim lands for Spain
   b. to obtain Asian silks and spices
   c. to use the wealth gained from the trip to recapture Jerusalem
   d. to discover the "New World"

3. What was the most likely reason why the Greenland settlement ended in the 14th century?
   a. Settlers returned to Scandinavia with riches from the seal-fur trade.
   b. Settlers died of starvation after the climate changed.
   c. Settlers migrated to Canada to start new settlements.
   d. Settlers moved back to Iceland because they ran out of firewood.

4. How did Columbus learn that Venezuela was part of a continent?
   a. He found the mouth of a large river.
   b. He sailed around the entire continent.
   c. He was told by the native people who lived there.
   d. He studied maps of the region that other explorers had made.

## B. CAUSE AND EFFECT

**This chart shows a cause-effect chain. Complete the chart by adding either a cause or an effect.**

| CAUSE | CAUSE/EFFECT | EFFECT |
|---|---|---|
| 5. _____ | He gave England a claim to the mainland of North America. | This led to the founding of the English colonies. |
| Columbus needed the backing of the Spanish monarchs. | He appealed to their religious beliefs. | 6. _____ |
| 7. _____ | The pope drew a line down what he thought was the center of the Atlantic Ocean. | Portugal became the ruler of Brazil. |

## C. ANALYZING THE ROLE OF CHANCE IN HISTORY

Write a paragraph in which you describe how America got its name. Explain how chance played a role in the naming. Use a separate sheet of paper.

# CHAPTER 11

# SAILORS, SUGAR, AND SLAVES: HOW EUROPEAN VOYAGES CHANGED ASIA AND AFRICA   PAGES 152–164

**FOR HOMEWORK**

Student Study Guide pages 51–54

## CHAPTER SUMMARY

Portuguese mariners expanded their control of sea trade during the 16th century, and established fortified trading posts along the coasts of Africa, India, and southeast Asia. They later became trading partners with Japan and China, which continued after Spain came to rule Portugal in 1580. The market for sugar and its production led to a steady increase in the slave trade, and formed the triangle trade between West Africa, Europe, and the Americas.

## PERFORMANCE OBJECTIVES

- ▶ To understand the difficulties of life at sea in the 16th century
- ▶ To describe how Portugal worked to dominate sea trade
- ▶ To explain the economic and human factors involved in sugar production
- ▶ To describe the growth of the slave trade between West Africa, Europe, and the Americas

## BUILDING BACKGROUND

Create a web to describe what life at sea might have been like during the 16th century. Guide students to think about food supplies, personal hygiene, and the perils of weather. Tell students that in Chapter 11 they will learn more about the lives of 16th-century sailors and about the impact of sea trade around the world.

## VOCABULARY

**contract**  a legal agreement between two or more people

**monotonous**  unvarying; dull in a repetitious way

**malnutrition**  poor nourishment, due to an insufficient or poor diet

**dominate**  to control by superior authority or power

**cultivation**  the act of growing and improving a crop

**refining**  processing something to make it pure

**plantations**  a large estate or farm on which crops are grown and harvested

**racist**  believing that one's race or ethnic background is superior

As needed, have students consult the glossary to define the following terms: *cochineal insects, maroons, ship biscuit, triangle trade.*

## WORKING WITH PRIMARY SOURCES

Point out the quotation from Sir John Hawkins on Student Edition page 161. Discuss what his words reveal about his attitude towards West Africans. Hawkins, a cousin of Sir Francis Drake, was the first English slave trader. Have students use print and electronic resources to learn more about Hawkins and his role in British naval history. Allow time for them to share their findings.

## GEOGRAPHY CONNECTION

**Movement** Have students locate Portugal on a world map. Then have them scan information in the chapter and trace the path of Portuguese mariners as they worked to dominate sea trade during the 16th century.

## READING COMPREHENSION QUESTIONS

1. Why did the Chinese decide to allow trade with the Portuguese? (*China had begun trading for silver with Japan, and Japan had begun trading with Portugal. China decided that the well-armed Portuguese ships would provide safe transport for silver.*)

2. What happened in Portugal in 1580? How did this affect trading? (*Spain conquered Portugal in 1580. This made trading easier between the Americas, Asia, and Europe.*)

3. Why did slave trade increase as sugar plantations developed? (*Natives and Europeans refused to do the work, so thousands of slaves were brought from West Africa to work on the sugar plantations.*)

4. How was plantation slavery different from slavery practiced in other places and times? (*Slaves on plantations were almost all black, and white owners and managers believed that blacks were inferior, so racism made this slavery very different and even more cruel.*)

5. What was the triangle trade? (*trading in slaves, sugar, and other goods across the Atlantic Ocean among West Africa, Europe, and the Caribbean*)

## CRITICAL THINKING QUESTIONS

1. How were Portuguese ships different from other sailing vessels used in the Indian Ocean? What advantages did they provide? (*They were sturdier, carried more weapons, and could carry more cargo.*)

2. Why did sugar plantations develop in the Caribbean and Brazil? What factors complicated this endeavor? (*Sugar was in great demand and grew well in these southern climates. However, it required enormous, difficult labor, and all products and workers had to be brought to sugar plantations.*)

3. How do you think slavery on sugar plantations influenced historical events to follow, especially in the southern United States? (*Plantation slavery was seen as acceptable and profitable. However, it eventually became an enormous social issue and led to the Civil War in the United States.*)

## SOCIAL SCIENCES

**Economics** Sugar plantations in the Caribbean and Brazil produced just one product, and everything else needed to be brought in. Use this idea to lead a discussion about the costs and benefits of island economics.

## READING AND LANGUAGE ARTS

**Reading Nonfiction** Discuss how the author uses a fictional account to introduce historical events in this chapter. Have students analyze how it helps the reader imagine real-life experiences, and guide students to see how the author later contrasts these experiences with the lives of slaves on sugar plantations.

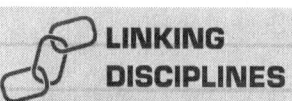

### THEN and NOW

By 1600, Brazil was the largest supplier of sugar to Europe. Today, Brazil is the world's top producer of sugar. Centered in São Paulo, new milling technologies allowed Brazil's sugar exports to double between 1996 and 2002.

### LINKING DISCIPLINES

**Health** Point out this description on Student Edition page 153 "... as the voyage wears on, your teeth get loose and your gums bleed." Explain that these are symptoms of scurvy, a disease caused by lack of vitamin C. Encourage students to learn more about the disease and how it came to be treated, beginning at *http://en.wikipedia.org/wiki/Scurvy*.

AN AGE OF VOYAGES, 1350–1600

## LITERATURE CONNECTION

There are numerous enjoyable books that will broaden students' knowledge of the impact of European voyages of discovery.

Dessalles, Pierre. *Sugar and Slavery, Family and Race: The Letters and Diary of Pierre Dessalles, Planter in Martinique, 1808-1856.* Baltimore: Johns Hopkins University Press, 1996. Nonfiction. The letters and diary of a sugar plantation manager describe the daily life and customs in 19th century Martinique.
**ADVANCED**

Lester, Julius. *To Be a Slave.* London: Puffin Books, 2000. Nonfiction. The reminiscences of former slaves reveal the feelings of those whose lives were devastated by the practice of slavery in the Americas.
**AVERAGE**

## LITERACY TIPS

In addition to using the suggestions in the Supporting Learning and Extending Learning sections, refer back frequently to pages 16-19 for strategies and advice from a literacy coach.

## READING AND LANGUAGE ARTS CONTINUED

**Using Language** Have pairs of students scan Student Edition pages 152-155 for descriptive details the author provides about the lives of 16th-century sailors, and have them keep a list of details that they find especially effective or illuminating in their history journals. Discuss how the details they identified help them to create a mental image of the sailors' lives.

## WRITING

**Narrative Letter** Have students choose the point of view of someone directly or indirectly involved in the establishment of sugar plantations in the Caribbean, such as a plantation owner or manager, an enslaved worker, a maroon, or a missionary. Have students write a letter that narrates and details their experiences.

## SUPPORTING LEARNING

**English Language Learners** Point out the phrases *hanging around* and *wash down your meals* on Student Edition page 153. Explain that these phrases are idioms that mean something different from what the words actually say. Group students of varying proficiency and have them look for idioms in the fictional account on pages 152-155. Then have groups share and explain the idioms they've found.

**Struggling Readers** As they read each paragraph or section, have students write questions they think a teacher would ask, such as; *How did Portuguese traders try to dominate sea trade?* After reading, have pairs of students share and answer each other's questions. Later, form small groups to share and discuss the questions and the chapter ideas they address.

## EXTENDING LEARNING

**Enrichment** Invite students to research narratives and images that illuminate the middle passage of the slave trade, and display or share their findings with the class. Have students examine Tom Feelings's pictorial essay on the middle passage at *www.juneteenth.com/middlep.htm.*

**Extension** Have students role-play representatives from Portugal, Japan, and China and present a discussion that describes how the lands became trading partners. Use the activity to assess students' understanding of the impact of trade in the 16th century.

CHAPTER 11

**NAME**            **DATE**

## THE TRIANGLE TRADE, 1650

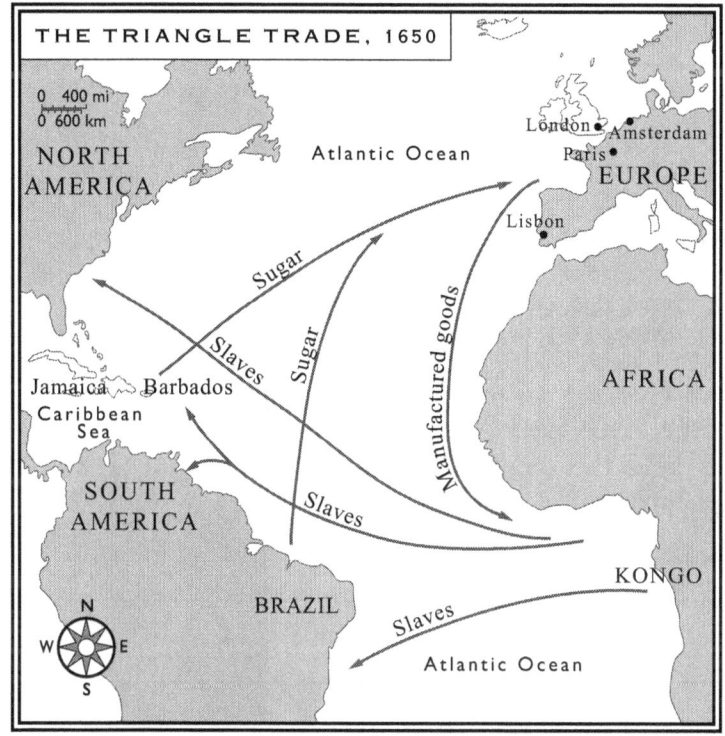

**Directions**

Use the map to answer the questions that follow.

1. Name the places to which slaves from Africa were taken.

2. Which one of those journeys appears to have been the longest?

3. From where did Europe get sugar?

4. Why do you think Europe sent manufactured goods to Africa?

5. Use the scale of miles to tell about how far slave ships traveled from Kongo to Brazil.

CHAPTER 11 BLM      AN AGE OF VOYAGES, 1350–1600      **89**

## WRECKING THE PLACE

**Directions**

The following text is from *The Medieval & Early Modern World Primary Sources and Reference Volume,* pages 74–75. This account, probably written by a German traveler on a Portuguese ship, describes the pillaging of the East African cities of Kilwa and Mombasa in 1505. Read the passage with a partner and answer the questions that follow.

> The Grand-Captain ordered that the town should be sacked and that each man should carry off to his ship whatever he found: so that at the end there would be a division of the spoil, each man to receive a twentieth of what he found. The same rule was made for gold, silver, and pearls. Then everyone started to plunder the town and to search the houses, forcing open the doors with axes and iron bars. There was a large quantity of cotton cloth for Sofala in the town, for the whole coast gets its cotton cloth from here. So the Grand-Captain got a good share of the trade of Sofala for himself. A large quantity of rich silk and gold embroidered clothes was seized, and carpets also; one of these which was without equal for beauty, was sent to the King of Portugal together with many other valuables.

1. Who profited from the sacking of these East African cities?

2. Why do you think the Grand-Captain "got a good share of the trade of Sofala for himself"?

3. How does this passage add to what you learned in Chapter 11 about how the Portuguese came to dominate sea trade during the 16th century?

4. Review Student Edition pages 156–157. How does the response of the Chinese to the Portuguese differ from this passage? What might explain this difference?

NAME _____ DATE _____

## A. MULTIPLE CHOICE

**Circle the letter of the best answer for each question.**

1. Which of the following describes how the Portuguese came to dominate sea trade during the 16th century?
   a. They used their sailing and navigation skills to provide goods more quickly.
   b. They worked with African and Indian allies to attack Japan and China.
   c. They provided sugar and slaves from Africa to Japan and China.
   d. They used force and fortified trading posts to control sea traffic.

2. Why did sugar plantations develop in the Caribbean and Brazil?
   a. Europeans wanted to control the supply of sugar to Japan and China.
   b. Sugar was in demand and these lands had the right growing climate.
   c. Sugar production was an inexpensive way to support their economies.
   d. Europeans used the native populations to supply sugar to Europe.

3. Who were "maroons" and what did they do?
   a. These escaped slaves formed communities where they could be free.
   b. They were people taken forcibly from Africa to work as slaves.
   c. They were native peoples who worked with slaves to sabotage plantations.
   d. They were Caribbean natives who worked as overseers on sugar plantations.

4. What made plantation slavery different from slavery that had existed in other parts of the world?
   a. Slaves on plantations were not paid for their labor.
   b. African slaves were seen by many people as inferior and less than human.
   c. Slaves on plantations were forced to do work that natives would not do.
   d. The children of slaves became the property of plantation owners.

## B. POINT OF VIEW

**Answer in complete sentences the following questions about plantation slavery.**

5. How did the way plantation owners treated their slaves reflect the way they viewed them?
   _____
   _____
   _____
   _____

6. What point of view did Catholic and Protestant churches have toward slavery?
   _____
   _____
   _____
   _____

## C. COMPARE AND CONTRAST

How did the lives of young boys who were placed in the service of ships' captains compare with the lives of African children enslaved on sugar plantations? On a separate sheet of paper, write a short essay in which you compare and contrast the lives of these children.

# CHAPTER 12

# GERMS, SILVER, AND BLOOD: NEW WORLD CONQUESTS AND GLOBAL CONNECTIONS
PAGES 165–179

**FOR HOMEWORK**
Student Study Guide pages 55–58

## CHAPTER SUMMARY

Spanish conqueror Hernán Cortés arrived in the Aztec capital of what is now Mexico in 1519. Two years later, Cortés ruled the entire Aztec Empire. In Peru, a similar pattern occurred when Francisco Pizarro reached the Inca capital of Cuzco in 1533. Culture in the Americas changed as the population of mestizos grew. The Columbian Exchange harmed people through the spread of new diseases, but it brought benefits, such as the exchange of crops and animals.

## PERFORMANCE OBJECTIVES

▶ To explain how the Aztec and Inca empires were defeated by the Spanish
▶ To understand the impact of missionaries on Christianity and the diffusion of Christianity from Europe to other parts of the world
▶ To describe the exchanges of plants, animals, technology, culture, and ideas among Europe, Africa, Asia, and the Americas

## BUILDING BACKGROUND

Ask students to define *conquest*. Invite them to list the possible effects of a conquest on both the conquerors and the conquered. Suggest they think of changes in the societies' culture, economics, and government. Keep the list on display, and remind students to refer to it as they read. Tell them that they will read about the effects of the Spanish conquest of the Americas.

## VOCABULARY

**conquest** defeating by the use of force
**epidemic** a disease affecting many people at the same time
**ally** one in a close association with another
**mission** a building that houses people who hope to spread religious beliefs
**revenue** the income from a particular source
**baroque** a style in art and architecture, marked by elaborate ornamentation

### CAST OF CHARACTERS

**Pizarro** (pih-ZAHR-roh), **Francisco** adventurer who conquered the Inca Empire

**Atahualpa** (ah-tuh-WAHL-pah) Inca leader killed during Pizarro's conquest

## WORKING WITH PRIMARY SOURCES

Direct students' attention to the Aztec account of Hernán Cortés's conquest of Mexico on Student Edition pages 168–169. Discuss how the passage helps historians get a better understanding of the experiences of the Aztecs during this time. Discuss how an account written from Cortés's point of view would differ.

### GEOGRAPHY CONNECTION

**Interaction** As students read about the Columbian Exchange on Student Edition page 179, have them use a world map to trace the path of trade goods among Asia, the Americas, Europe, and Africa. Use the activity to assess students' understanding of the impact of the Columbian Exchange.

### READING COMPREHENSION QUESTIONS

1. Why did the Aztecs view warfare as a religious duty? (*They believed that the sun god demanded the sacrifice of captured enemy warriors to maintain his energy so that crops would grow and life would continue.*)
2. How did Hernán Cortés defeat the Aztecs? (*He had the help of local allies, who were enemies of the Aztecs, and he had weapons that used gunpowder. In addition, Europeans brought diseases that killed and weakened local populations.*)
3. What did the Incas demand from the people they conquered? (*tribute and taxes in the form of crops and forced labor*)
4. Who was Francisco Pizarro? (*He was a Spanish adventurer who defeated the Incas and became the governor of Peru.*)
5. In what way was silver important to the European economy? (*Most of the buying and selling and tax-paying was done with coins, and most of the coins were silver.*)

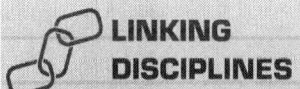

**THEN and NOW**

Today Mexico and Peru are leading producers of silver. Silver has electrical, mechanical, optical, photographic, and medicinal uses. Mexican and Peruvian silver jewelry is sold throughout the world.

### CRITICAL THINKING QUESTIONS

1. How did the Incas' excellent road system help them before the Spanish conquest and harm them during it? (*Before the Spanish conquest, the Incas used the road system to maintain their empire: transporting food and for messengers and armies to move swiftly. During the Spanish conquest, infectious diseases traveled quickly on the roads.*)
2. How did Christianity spread in New Spain? (*Missionaries set up missions and tried to convert native people.*)
3. What was the Spanish government's economic relationship to the private investors of silver mines? (*The Spanish government granted the rights to mine silver to private investors in exchange for 20 percent of the silver they mined.*)
4. How did trade affect the spread of crops? Give an example. (*Possible answer: Sugarcane from Asia was brought to the Americas, and chocolate was taken to Spain. People began drinking sweetened chocolate.*)

### SOCIAL SCIENCES

**Economics** Direct interested students to research the global trade of people and goods during the "triangle trade" and the Columbian Exchange. Suggest they make a detailed diagram of their findings, or present what they learn in a skit. Useful websites include www.bartleby.com/65/sl/slavery.html and www.rit.edu/~africa/diaspora/mapPg1.shtml.

### READING AND LANGUAGE ARTS

**Reading Nonfiction** The chapter discusses four major topics: the conquest of the Aztecs, the conquest of the Incas, life under the Spanish colonization, and the Columbian Exchange. Have students identify the main idea and details of each section.

**LINKING DISCIPLINES**

**Science** Invite interested students to research the spread of smallpox or another of the infectious diseases discussed in the chapter. Suggest that they focus on understanding its life cycle and method of reproduction. Tell students to create a poster to use as part of an oral presentation to the class.

AN AGE OF VOYAGES, 1350–1600

### LITERATURE CONNECTION

There are numerous enjoyable books that will broaden students' knowledge of the Inca and Aztec empires, both before and after Spanish conquests.

Clark, Ann Nolan. *Secret of the Andes.* London: Puffin Books, 1976. Historical Fiction. A llama herder learns about the traditions of his Inca ancestors. EASY

Guadiano, Andrea. *Azteca: Story of a Jaguar Warrior.* Lanham, MD: Roberts Rinehart Publishers, 1992. Nonfiction. The author examines life just before and during the conquest of Tenochtitlan. AVERAGE

Hemming, John. *The Conquest of the Inca.* San Diego: Harvest/HBJ, 2003. Nonfiction. The Inca's struggles against the Spanish are detailed in this comprehensive work. ADVANCED

### LITERACY TIPS

In addition to using the suggestions in the Supporting Learning and Extending Learning sections, refer back frequently to pages 16–19 for strategies and advice from a literacy coach.

## READING AND LANGUAGE ARTS CONTINUED

**Using Language** Point out this sentence in the last paragraph on page 166: "They repaid this welcome by fighting their hosts, and capturing and killing the emperor." Define irony, and elicit why this sentence is ironic *(there is an incongruity between what might have been expected—gratefulness to the hosts—and what actually happened—violence)*. Have students make up their own ironic statements about events in the chapter.

## WRITING

**Write a Summary** Tell students to write a summary of the chapter. Remind them to include the main ideas and the most significant details and to use their own words. Suggest they read aloud their drafts with a partner before revising them.

## SUPPORTING LEARNING

**English Language Learners** Help students understand the economic terms in the chapter by role-playing economic exchanges. For example, one student can be a government official and an English-fluent partner can be a silver mine investor. Suggest that they begin with these terms: *investors, revenue,* and *taxes.*

**Struggling Readers** Direct students to meet with a partner to discuss how the Spanish conquests of the Aztec and the Inca empires were similar and different. Remind them to look for signal words in the text, such as *both* and *like*.

## EXTENDING LEARNING

**Enrichment** The Aztecs had specific religious beliefs that condoned, or allowed, human sacrifice. Have students research the Aztec religion and present what they learned in an oral report. They might look at such sites as *http://philtar.uscm.ac.uk/encyclopedia/latam/aztec.html.*

**Extension** Have students find examples of mestizo or indigenous (native) culture in Mexico and Peru today. Suggest that they look at such cultural features as language, religion, art, and music. Invite them to prepare an oral report and to make a multimedia display that includes recordings and photographs.

**NAME**            **DATE**

## THE AZTEC AND INCA EMPIRES, 1500

**Directions**

Use the map to answer the questions that follow.

1. What were the two main cities of the Aztec Empire?

2. What was the dominant physical feature of the Inca Empire?

3. Why do you think Acapulco might have been a port city?

4. What is the approximate distance between Lima and Cuzco?

5. Why do you think it was easier for the Spanish conquerors to reach Tenochtitlan than Cuzco?

CHAPTER BLM 12 — An Age of Voyages, 1350–1600

NAME                                    DATE

# IT WAS HARSH

**Directions**

The following text is from *The Medieval & Early Modern World Primary Sources and Reference Volume,* pages 77–79. It is an excerpt from Aztec writers, who composed a song of grief after Hernán Cortés's siege of 1521. Read the excerpt with a partner, and answer the questions that follow. If necessary, check a dictionary for help with unfamiliar words.

> And all this happened among us. We saw it. We lived through it with
> an astonishment worthy of tears and of pity for the pain we suffered.
> On the roads lie broken shafts and torn hair,
> houses are roofless, homes are stained red,
> worms swarm in the streets, walls are spattered with brains.
> The water is reddish, like dyed water;
> we drink it so, we even drink brine;
> the water we drink is full of saltpetre.
> The wells are crammed with adobe bricks.
> Whatever was still alive was kept between shields, like precious
> treasure, between shields, until it was eaten.
> We chewed on hard tzompantli wood, brackish zacatl fodder, chunks
> of adobe, lizards, vermin, dust and worms.

**1.** What is the point of view of the writer of this account of the siege? How can you tell?

_____
_____
_____

**2.** How does knowing the Aztec point of view help you understand this time in history?

_____
_____
_____

**3.** What were the main difficulties faced by the Aztecs?

_____
_____
_____

**4.** How can you tell that food was scarce during the siege?

_____
_____
_____

# CHAPTER TEST 12

**AN AGE OF VOYAGES, 1350–1600**

## A. MULTIPLE CHOICE

**Circle the letter of the best answer for each question.**

1. Why did Hernán Cortés originally want to explore the east coast of Mexico?
   - **a.** to find gold
   - **b.** to locate a water route to Asia
   - **c.** to set up Christian missions
   - **d.** to open silver mines

2. Which of the following was **not** a reason why Hernán Cortés was able to defeat the Aztecs?
   - **a.** European diseases had weakened the Aztecs.
   - **b.** The Spanish troops had access to gunpowder.
   - **c.** The enemies of the Aztecs joined the Spanish troops.
   - **d.** The Spanish forces outnumbered the Aztecs.

3. How did missionaries support local cultures?
   - **a.** They gave them legal advice on how to regain their land.
   - **b.** They preserved local traditions and customs.
   - **c.** They taught them how to read in their native languages.
   - **d.** They protected them from plantation owners.

4. Which was a major change in culture in the Americas by the early 1600s?
   - **a.** Mestizos began to dominate the population of Brazil.
   - **b.** People of Spanish ancestry outnumbered the mestizos in Mexico.
   - **c.** The governments in Latin America supported equal rights for all cultures.
   - **d.** Slavery was outlawed throughout South America and Central America.

## B. CAUSE AND EFFECT

**Complete the chart to show the cause-effect relationships.**

| CAUSE | CAUSE/EFFECT | EFFECT |
|---|---|---|
| Europeans brought diseases with them to the Americas. | 5. _____ | The conquerors had an easier time taking over empires. |
| 6. _____ | People had an easier time traveling through the Andes. | Deadly diseases spread more easily, too. |
| Europeans brought domesticated animals to the Americas and took back new crops. | Nutrition was improved around the world. | 7. _____ |

## C. FOLLOWING THE SEQUENCE OF EVENTS

9. On a separate sheet of paper, write an essay about the mining operations in Peru. Tell how they changed over time as mine owners looked for solutions to labor problems

**WRAP-UP TEST**
AN AGE OF VOYAGES, 1350–1600

**NAME**             **DATE**

**Directions**
Answer each of the following questions. Use additional paper if necessary

**1.** Write a paragraph that describes how the Ottoman Empire's policy of religious tolerance contributed cultural blending within Muslim civilizations.

_____
_____
_____
_____
_____
_____
_____
_____

**2.** On a separate sheet of paper, use the main idea map graphic organizer to show the details that support the following main idea: Cities grew along trade routes in the 15th and 16th centuries.

**3.** Write one or two paragraphs to explain how Zheng He's voyages helped to end China's isolation from Europe and Africa.

_____
_____
_____
_____
_____
_____
_____
_____

**4.** Portugal's Prince Henry "the Navigator" sponsored several voyages in the 15th century. Write a paragraph to describe how these voyages made Portugal a leader in trade and exploration.

_____
_____
_____
_____
_____
_____
_____
_____

**5.** The Spanish conquered both the Aztec and the Inca Empires. On a separate sheet of paper, make a Venn diagram to show how the conquests were alike and how they were different.

**NAME** _____ **DATE** _____

**6.** Write a paragraph to explain two effects of trade along the Silk Road.

_____
_____
_____
_____
_____
_____
_____
_____

**7.** Spain and Portugal remained Catholic during and after the Protestant Reformation. Write a paragraph to explain the effects of the countries' religious beliefs on the New World.

_____
_____
_____
_____
_____
_____
_____
_____

**8.** Write a paragraph to describe the impact of Ignatius Loyola and the Jesuits on the Protestant Reformation.

_____
_____
_____
_____
_____
_____
_____

**9.** Map makers in the 16th century did more than show the geography of the New World. Write a paragraph in which you explain how map makers had a role in naming the New World.

_____
_____
_____
_____
_____
_____
_____

**10.** Choose one product or exchange that occurred as part of the Triangle Trade. On a separate sheet of paper, use a two-column chart with the headings *Economic Changes* and *Social Changes* to list examples of the impact of the product or exchange.

# SCORING RUBRIC

The reproducibles on the following pages have been adapted from this rubric for use as handouts and a student self-scoring activity, with added focus on planning, cooperation, revision and presentation. You may wish to tailor the self-scoring activity—for example, asking students to comment on how low scores could be improved, or focusing only on specific rubric points. Use the Library/Media Center Research Log to help students focus and evaluate their research for projects and assignments.

As with any rubric, you should introduce and explain the rubric before students begin their assignments. The more thoroughly your students understand how they will be evaluated, the better prepared they will be to produce projects that fulfill your expectations.

| | ORGANIZATION | CONTENT | ORAL/WRITTEN CONVENTIONS | GROUP PARTICIPATION |
|---|---|---|---|---|
| **4** | • Clearly addresses all parts of the writing task.<br>• Demonstrates a clear understanding of purpose and audience.<br>• Maintains a consistent point of view, focus, and organizational structure, including the effective use of transitions.<br>• Includes a clearly presented central idea with relevant facts, details, and/or explanations. | • Demonstrates that the topic was well researched.<br>• Uses only information that was essential and relevant to the topic.<br>• Presents the topic thoroughly and accurately.<br>• Reaches reasonable conclusions clearly based on evidence. | • Contains few, if any, errors in grammar, punctuation, capitalization, or spelling.<br>• Uses a variety of sentence types.<br>• Speaks clearly, using effective volume and intonation. | • Demonstrated high levels of participation and effective decision making.<br>• Planned well and used time efficiently.<br>• Demonstrated ability to negotiate opinions fairly and reach compromise when needed.<br>• Utilized effective visual aids. |
| **3** | • Addresses all parts of the writing task.<br>• Demonstrates a general understanding of purpose and audience.<br>• Maintains a mostly consistent point of view, focus, and organizational structure, including the effective use of some transitions.<br>• Presents a central idea with mostly relevant facts, details, and/or explanations. | • Demonstrates that the topic was sufficiently researched.<br>• Uses mainly information that was essential and relevant to the topic.<br>• Presents the topic accurately but leaves some aspects unexplored.<br>• Reaches reasonable conclusions loosely related to evidence. | • Contains some errors in grammar, punctuation, capitalization, or spelling.<br>• Uses a variety of sentence types.<br>• Speaks somewhat clearly, using effective volume and intonation. | • Demonstrated good participation and decision making with few distractions.<br>• Planning and used its time acceptably.<br>• Demonstrated ability to negotiate opinions and compromise with little aggression or unfairness. |
| **2** | • Addresses only parts of the writing task.<br>• Demonstrates little understanding of purpose and audience.<br>• Maintains an inconsistent point of view, focus, and/or organizational structure, which may include ineffective or awkward transitions that do not unify important ideas.<br>• Suggests a central idea with limited facts, details, and/or explanations. | • Demonstrates that the topic was minimally researched.<br>• Uses a mix of relevant and irrelevant information.<br>• Presents the topic with some factual errors and leaves some aspects unexplored.<br>• Reaches conclusions that do not stem from evidence presented in the project. | • Contains several errors in grammar, punctuation, capitalization, or spelling. These errors may interfere with the reader's understanding of the writing.<br>• Uses little variety in sentence types.<br>• Speaks unclearly or too quickly. May interfere with the audience's understanding of the project. | • Demonstrated uneven participation or was often off-topic. Task distribution was lopsided.<br>• Did not show a clear plan for the project, and did not use time well.<br>• Allowed one or two opinions to dominate the activity, or had trouble reaching a fair consensus. |
| **1** | • Addresses only one part of the writing task.<br>• Demonstrates no understanding of purpose and audience.<br>• Lacks a point of view, focus, organizational structure, and transitions that unify important ideas.<br>• Lacks a central idea but may contain marginally related facts, details, and/or explanations. | • Demonstrates that the topic was poorly researched.<br>• Does not discriminate relevant from irrelevant information.<br>• Presents the topic incompletely, with many factual errors.<br>• Did not reach conclusions. | • Contains serious errors in grammar, punctuation, capitalization, or spelling. These errors interfere with the reader's understanding of the writing.<br>• Uses no sentence variety.<br>• Speaks unclearly. The audience must struggle to understand the project. | • Demonstrated poor participation by the majority of the group. Tasks were completed by a small minority.<br>• Failed to show planning or effective use of time.<br>• Was dominated by a single voice, or allowed hostility to derail the project. |

**NAME** _____  **PROJECT** _____

**DATE** _____

| ORGANIZATION & FOCUS | CONTENT | ORAL/WRITTEN CONVENTIONS | GROUP PARTICIPATION |
|---|---|---|---|
| | | | |

## COMMENTS AND SUGGESTIONS

## UNDERSTANDING YOUR SCORE

**Organization:** Your project should be clear, focused on a main idea, and organized. You should use details and facts to support your main idea.

**Content:** You should use strong research skills. Your project should be thorough and accurate.

**Oral/Written Conventions:** For writing projects, you should use good composition, grammar, punctuation, and spelling, with a good variety of sentence types. For oral projects, you should engage the class using good public speaking skills.

**Group Participation:** Your group should cooperate fairly and use its time well to plan, assign and revise the tasks involved in the project.

**NAME** _____  **GROUP MEMBERS** _____

_____

_____

_____

Use this worksheet to describe your project by finishing the sentences below.
For individual projects and writing assignments, use the "How I did" section.
For group projects, use both "How I did" and "How we did" sections.

The purpose of this project is to :

[                                                                              ]

Scoring Key = **4** – extremely well
**3** – well
**2** – could have been better
**1** – not well at all

## HOW I DID

I understood the purpose and requirements for this project…

I planned and organized my time and work…

This project showed clear organization that emphasized the central idea…

I supported my point with details and description…

I polished and revised this project…

I utilized correct grammar and good writing/speaking style…

Overall, this project met its purpose…

## HOW WE DID

We divided up tasks…

We cooperated and listened to each other…

We talked through what we didn't understand…

We used all our time to make this project the best it could be…

Overall, as a group we worked together…

I contributed and cooperated with the team…

# LIBRARY/ MEDIA CENTER RESEARCH LOG

**NAME** _____  **DUE DATE** _____

**What I Need to Find**

**Places I Know to Look**

**Brainstorm**: Other Sources and Places to Look

I need to use:
- ☐ primary sources.
- ☐ secondary

## WHAT I FOUND

**Title/Author/Location (call # or URL)**

|  | Book/Periodical | Website | Other | Primary Source | Secondary Source | How I Found it: Suggestion | Library Catalog | Browsing | Internet Search | Web link | Rate each source from 1 (low) to 4 (high) in the categories below — helpful | relevant |
|---|---|---|---|---|---|---|---|---|---|---|---|---|
| ____ | ☐ | ☐ | ☐ | ☐ | ☐ | ☐ | ☐ | ☐ | ☐ | ☐ | ____ | ____ |
| ____ | ☐ | ☐ | ☐ | ☐ | ☐ | ☐ | ☐ | ☐ | ☐ | ☐ | ____ | ____ |
| ____ | ☐ | ☐ | ☐ | ☐ | ☐ | ☐ | ☐ | ☐ | ☐ | ☐ | ____ | ____ |
| ____ | ☐ | ☐ | ☐ | ☐ | ☐ | ☐ | ☐ | ☐ | ☐ | ☐ | ____ | ____ |
| ____ | ☐ | ☐ | ☐ | ☐ | ☐ | ☐ | ☐ | ☐ | ☐ | ☐ | ____ | ____ |
| ____ | ☐ | ☐ | ☐ | ☐ | ☐ | ☐ | ☐ | ☐ | ☐ | ☐ | ____ | ____ |

# GRAPHIC ORGANIZERS

## GUIDELINES

Reproducibles of seven different graphic organizers are provided on the following pages. These give your students a variety of ways to sort and order all the information they are receiving in this course. Use the organizers for homework assignments, classroom activities, tests, small group projects, and as ways to help the students take notes as they read.

1. Determine which graphic organizers work best for the content you are teaching. Some are useful for identifying main ideas and details; others work better for making comparisons, and so on.

2. Graphic organizers help students focus on the central points of the lesson while leaving out irrelevant details.

3. Use graphic organizers to give a visual picture of the key ideas you are teaching.

4. Graphic organizers can help students recall important information. Suggest students use them to study for tests.

5. Graphic organizers provide a visual way to show the connections between different content areas.

6. Graphic organizers can enliven traditional lesson plans and encourage greater interactivity within the classroom.

7. Apply graphic organizers to give students a concise, visual way to break down complex ideas.

8. Encourage students to use graphic organizers to identify patterns and clarify their ideas.

9. Graphic organizers stimulate creative thinking in the classroom, in small groups, and for the individual student.

10. Help students determine which graphic organizers work best for their purposes, and encourage them to use graphic organizers collaboratively whenever they can.

11. Help students customize graphic organizers as particular exercises dictate: e.g., more or fewer boxes, lines, or blanks than appear.

# OUTLINE

**MAIN IDEA:** _____
_____
_____

    **DETAIL:** _____
    _____

    **DETAIL:** _____
    _____

    **DETAIL:** _____
    _____

**MAIN IDEA:** _____
_____
_____

    **DETAIL:** _____
    _____

    **DETAIL:** _____
    _____

    **DETAIL:** _____
    _____

Name _____ Date _____

# MAIN IDEA MAP

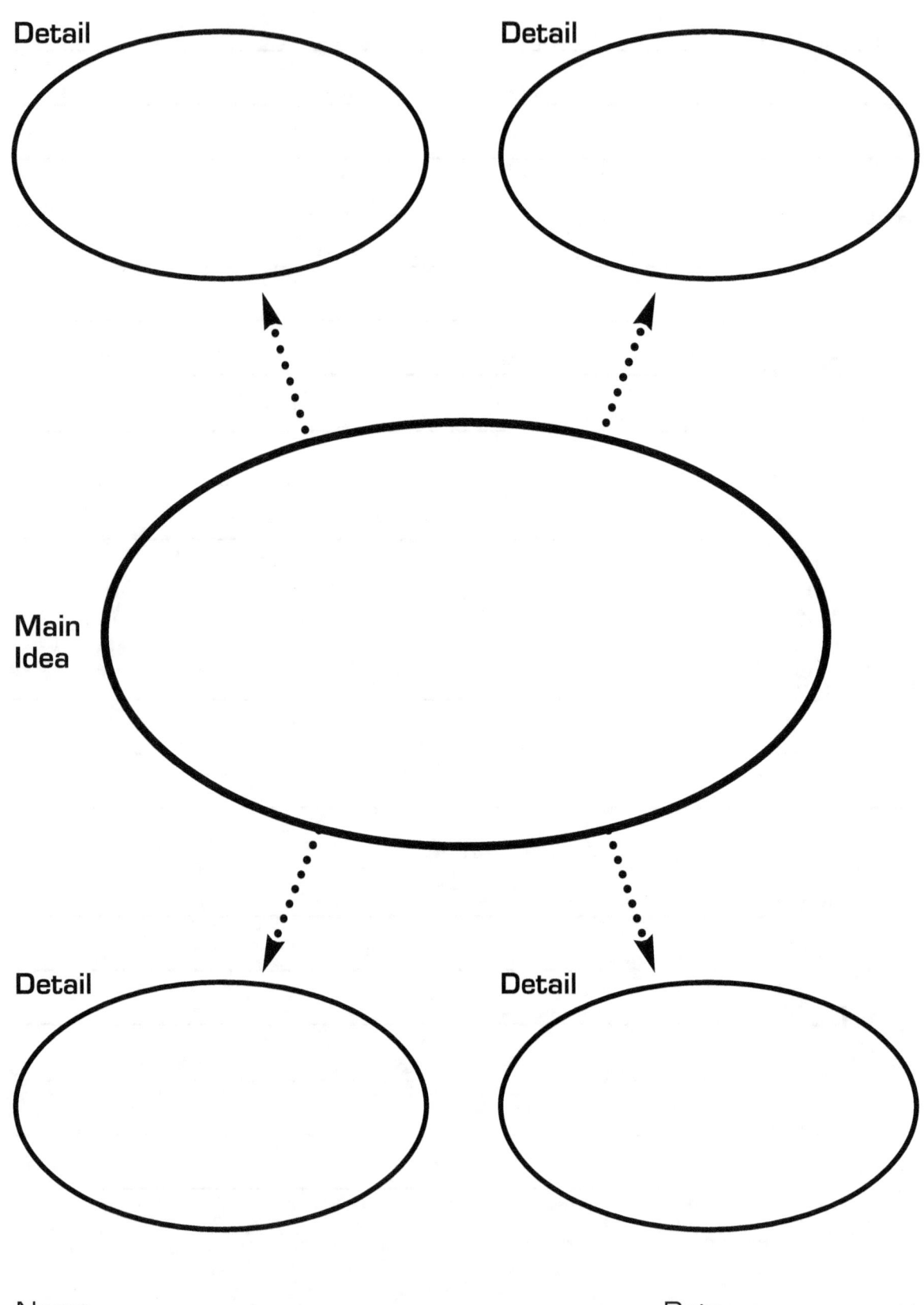

Name _____ Date _____

# K-W-L CHART

| K | W | L |
|---|---|---|
| What I Know | What I Want to Know | What I Learned |
|  |  |  |

Name _____  Date _____

# VENN DIAGRAM

Write differences in the circles. Write similarities where the circles overlap.

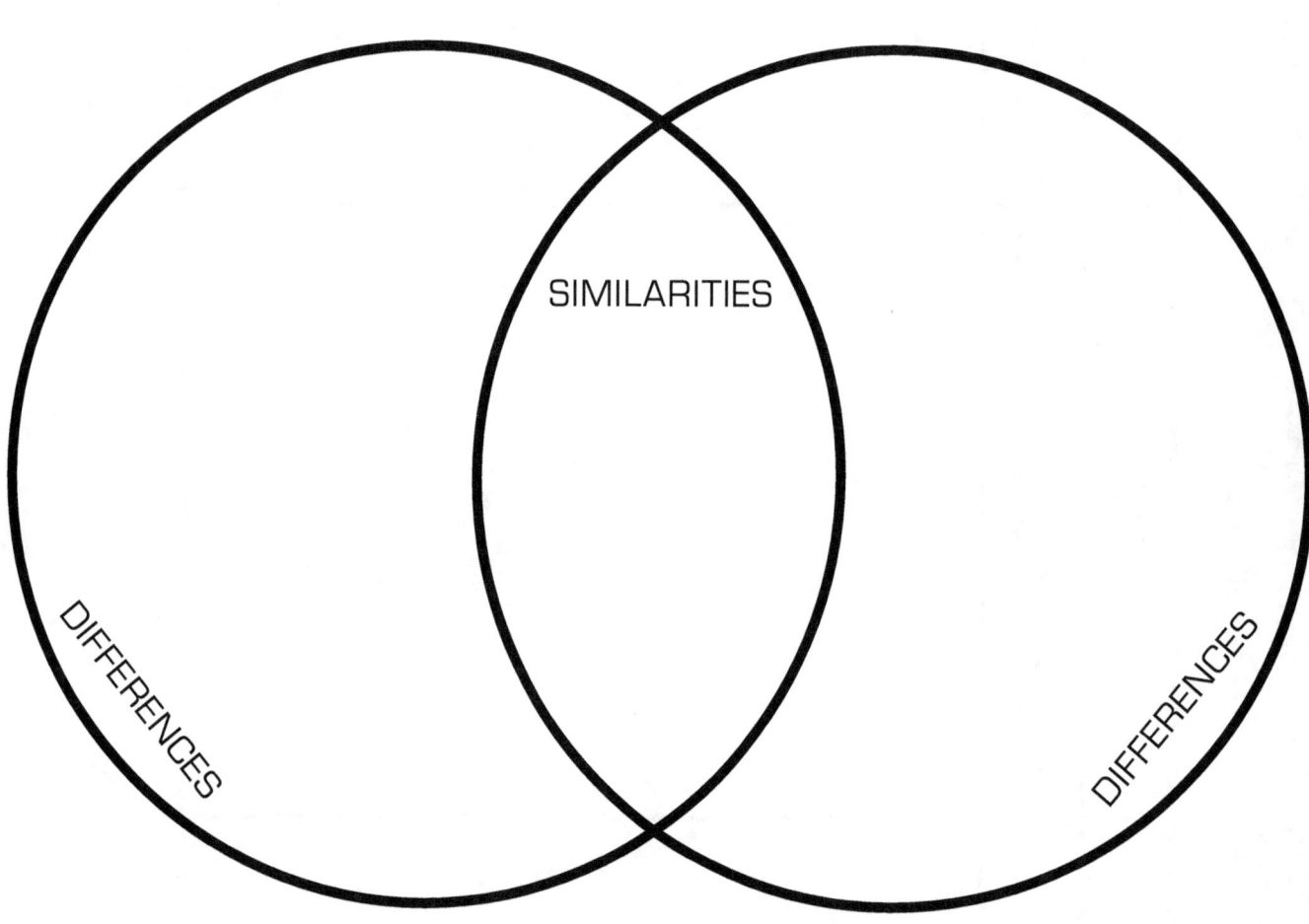

Name _____ Date _____

# TIMELINE

**DATE**

**EVENT** Draw lines to connect the event to the correct year on the timeline.

Name _____ Date

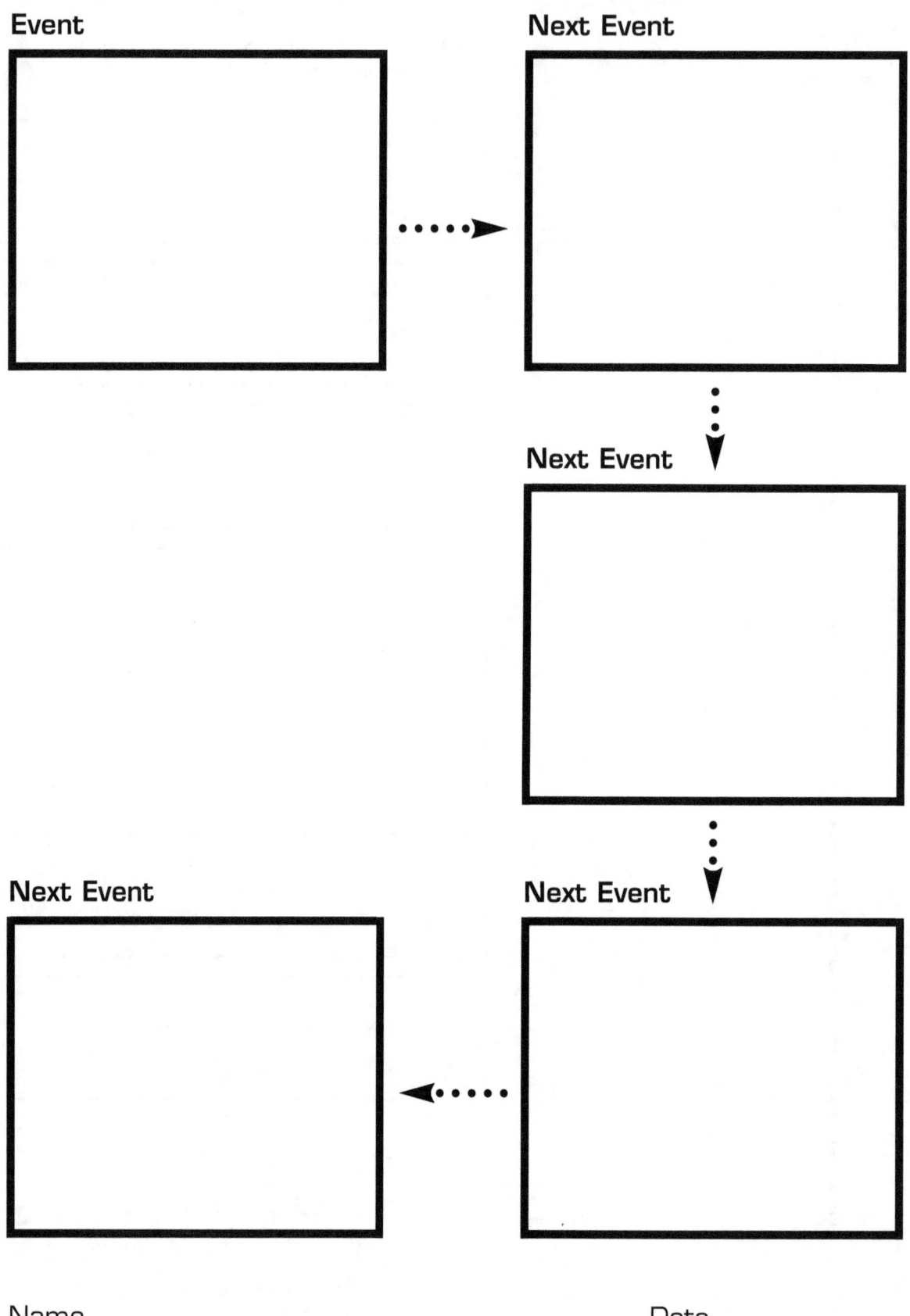

# T-CHART

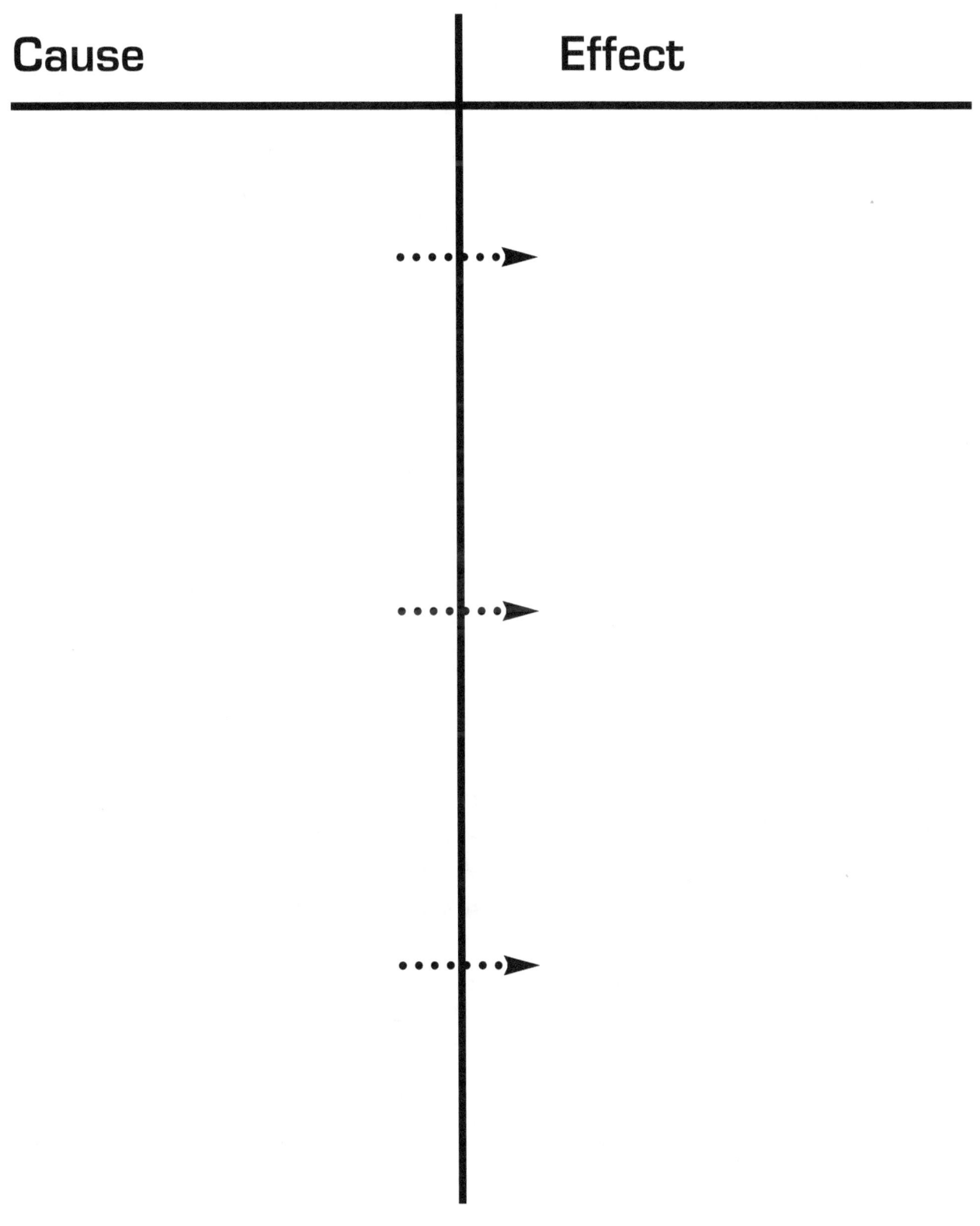

Name _____ Date _____

# ANSWER KEY

## CHAPTER 1
### BLACKLINE MASTER 1

1. It spread via the Silk Road, and it spread along a water route that first went through the South China Sea and then toward the Bay of Bengal.
2. about 2400 miles
3. in 1347
4. The plague spread along three routes to Baghdad: a land route from the Bay of Bengal to Baghdad, a water route from the Bay of Bengal to the Arabian Sea and on to Baghdad, and a land route from Mecca to Baghdad.
5. fifteen years

### BLACKLINE MASTER 2

1. The text illustrates that fleas were a common and recurring problem in people's homes.
2. Fleas in the home were probably a common problem. The husband warns his wife to be on the lookout for fleas in the summertime and tells her of three ways to catch them, one of which he, himself, has used successfully.
3. Possible answer: The second, because the fleas would get stuck in the glue or turpentine and be unable to get loose again.
4. Possible answer: It may have been written in response to a request for advice.

### CHAPTER TEST

A. 1. b 2. d 3. a 4. c

B. 5. Mongol armies catapulted plague-infected corpses into the city of Kaffa.

6. People thought the plague came from poisoned air.

7. The population dropped dramatically.

C. Students should describe one of the following routes. First route: Baghdad to Trebizond; from Trebizond across the Black Sea to Constantinople; from Constantinople via water to Venice. Second route: Baghdad to Damascus; from Damascus to the Mediterranean Sea, then via water to Venice.

## CHAPTER 2
### BLACKLINE MASTER 1

1. the Holy Roman Empire
2. the pope; the Papal States
3. The Italian Peninsula extended into the Mediterranean Sea, so it was a natural place for sea trade. It also was close to a number of countries by land routes.
4. They could then make their own decisions about trade without interference from government officials.
5. roughly 800 miles

### BLACKLINE MASTER 2

1. He addresses other artists, people such as historians, poets and mathematicians, and humans in general.
2. He says that writers and thinkers could not tell about things if they had not seen them with their eyes.
3. He probably means that artists, through their work, reflect the wonders and glories of God's creations.
4. He says that while the human body is wondrous in its construction, the soul within is even more marvelous and closer to God.

### CHAPTER TEST

A. 1. a 2. c 3. c 4. b 5. b

B. 1. Wealthy merchants gained political power to control Italian cities.

2. The wealthy merchant families supported artists and humanist ideas.

3. Humanist education and classical knowledge spread across Europe.

C. Students' essays should note that humanists were interested in individuals, especially those who had risen above their background to be powerful, brilliant, or unique. By making self-portraits and signing their works, artists were highlighting their individuality and uniqueness.

## CHAPTER 3
### BLACKLINE MASTER 1

1. It is directed to women. You can tell because the author is telling other women how to behave. She mentions the behavior expected of a wife.
2. Their duties included serving their parents-in-law, spinning, weaving, sewing clothes, and preparing sacrificial foods. To verify the information, you could read other historical accounts or view paintings made at the time that show ordinary women at work.
3. They are similar to other Confucian ideas that describe people's roles in society and how to show respect to others.
4. Students might say that the guidelines teach women to understand their role in society so they can work hard and contribute to the well-being of others.
5. Students' comparisons and contrasts should draw upon their understanding of Confucian ideas

### BLACKLINE MASTER 2

1. Possible answer: The author believes that young people should know their place in society and behave appropriately; he believes that people should not be boastful, even if they have unique talents or abilities; he believes that people should eat and speak appropriately.
2. Possible answer: Some young people may have broken the law by gambling, fighting, engaging in lawsuits, and dealing with salt privately.
3. Students should restate one of the sayings in their own words. They should identify it as an opinion, since it expresses a belief about how people should behave.
4. Ancient Confucian ideas stressed that people should know their place in the world, and these sayings reflect that belief.

### CHAPTER TEST

A. 1. a 2. c 3. d 4. a 5. c

B. 6. Mongol palaces were looted, Mongol names were taken out of court records, and Mongol jackets and shorter haircuts were replaced by traditional Chinese clothing.

7. Women had to obey their fathers, husbands, and sons.

8. They were an opportunity for bright commoners to get good government jobs.

9. Possible answer: China became wealthy through exporting popular goods, such as porcelain and lacquerware. China benefited from importing new crops, such as corn, to feed the growing population.

C. Students' paragraphs should show similarities between Renaissance Europe and Ming China, such as the following: In both societies, the economy grew, education focused on the classical past, and artists such as William Shakespeare and Tang Xianzu created new styles of art. Wealthy merchants, landowners, and political leaders purchased beautiful goods.

## CHAPTER 4
### BLACKLINE MASTER 1

Check student work against information in the text.

### BLACKLINE MASTER 2

1. He is totally against war. Students may or may not agree, but should support their answers with facts and reasons.
2. People thought the printing press was the devil's invention because it seemed unrealistically fast and powerful, spreading all kinds of ideas throughout Europe. Perhaps they also found the diversity and controversial nature of such ideas dangerous. Erasmus probably thought of the weapons of war as the "devil's art" because they are designed for only one purpose—to hurt and kill people.
3. He says that animals fight only to protect their young and to get food, while people fight for various selfish reasons such as ambition and anger. Students may or may not find such generalizations fair and accurate. All answers should be supported by facts and reasons.
4. Possible answer: Political and religious views, widely circulated through printed copies, could encourage populations to unite against what they perceive to be common enemies.

# ANSWER KEY

## CHAPTER TEST

A. 1. c  2. d  3. b  4. d

B. 5. A journeyman had to do a complicated printing job, his "masterpiece," and have it accepted by other printers.

6. The purpose of copyright laws is to prevent people from copying and stealing the original thoughts and works of others.

C. Essays and opinions will vary, but should be supported by facts and examples. Essays should clearly state the writer's opinion, and provide convincing arguments to support it.

## CHAPTER 5

### BLACKLINE MASTER 1

1. Russia
2. north to Denmark, Norway, Sweden and along the Baltic coastline; east through Poland; west and south through parts of Saxony
3. Catholicism
4. *Possible answer:* Religious conflicts might have continued in areas such as Saxony, with shared religions, or between bordering countries with opposing religions, such as France and England.
5. The map shows the colors for Muslim and for "Mixed Religiously."

### BLACKLINE MASTER 2

1. He probably wanted to convert people to his beliefs.
2. He believes that their souls will not profit, or benefit.
3. He believes that their souls will not be harmed, because a soul needs only the Word of God for its life and righteousness.
4. *Possible answer:* to make sure the desire for earthly things does not take over their lives and to show love to God
5. *Possible answer:* Perhaps he showed them a new way to obey God and protect their souls from harm.

### CHAPTER TEST

A. 1. b  2. c  3. a  4. d

B. 5. Rulers persecuted Christian groups whose ideas did not match theirs.

6. John Calvin reformed the government of Geneva, Switzerland.

7. Teresa of Avila was inspired by the Jesuits' achievements.

8. The Catholic hierarchy wanted to stop the spread of Calvinism.

C. *Possible answer:* Students should infer that many of the colonists left their homes in Europe due to religious persecution. As a result, the founders of the United States valued religious freedom.

## CHAPTER 6

### BLACKLINE MASTER 1

1. the Ottoman Empire
2. The Ottoman Empire controlled most of the land surrounding the Mediterranean Sea, except for the most northwest lands, such as Italy and Spain.
3. The Ottoman Empire; it controlled a larger land area and most of the lands and sea routes around the Mediterranean.
4. *Possible answer:* The area around the Indus and Ganga Rivers was probably heavily populated, since people tended to live near rivers for food, water, and transportation. The areas further to the north may not have been as attractive for the Mughals to conquer, and may have been more difficult to reach.
5. At the closest point, about 1,000 miles

### BLACKLINE MASTER 2

1. *Possible answer:* Akbar probably sees it as bad; he shows how this type of thinking leads to the formation of enemies, and says that it makes him feel doubtful.
2. *Possible answer:* He hoped to have listeners think about his words and consider ways to end intolerance.
3. *Possible answer:* They may have wanted to learn about others, to learn more about Akbar as emperor, or to understand his views on religious tolerance.
4. *Possible answer:* I think Akbar hopes that they will come to see that no religion is the mightiest and truest.
5. *Possible answer:* People would want their religion to be true so they could attain salvation. They would want it to be mighty because it was a time of religious wars.

## CHAPTER TEST

A. 1. b  2. d  3. d  4. a  5. c

B. *Possible answer:* Unlike rulers in western Europe who struggled to establish one set of religious beliefs above all others, the Ottoman and Mughal Empires both tolerated religious diversity in order to unify their people. However, both were gunpowder empires because they used new weapons and force to expand and maintain their lands and control.

## CHAPTER 7

### BLACKLINE MASTER 1

1. Both empires were located on rivers.
2. At its largest points, the Songhay Empire was about 500 miles wide and 700 miles from north to south. The Kingdom of Kongo was about 300 miles wide and 300 miles from north to south.
3. Traders from the south could reach the cities by traveling on the Niger River. The cities were fairly close together, which provided traders who crossed the Sahara more opportunities to buy and sell their products.
4. The Sahara Desert provided a natural barrier that was difficult for an invading army to cross.
5. The Congo River and the Atlantic Ocean made it easy for slave traders to transport and sell the people they enslaved.

### BLACKLINE MASTER 2

1. Rulers may have believed that when they spoke, they spoke for the entire government.
2. Elizabeth believed that she had the loyalty and good will of all her subjects, and had no reason to fear them.
3. She wanted to be near the battle when her troops fought, perhaps to prove her strength as a leader.
4. Elizabeth warned that she would fight any ruler who invaded her country.

### CHAPTER TEST

A. 1. b  2. c  3. d  4. a

B. 5. Many scholars fled the city of Timbuktu.

6. He used Islamic scholars as advisors, supported the building of mosques, and encouraged the writing of books on Muslim history and law.

7. It was not difficult for African people to accept Christian teachings.

C. Paragraphs will vary but students' opinions should be supported with details from the text. Students may mention Elizabeth's skills as a negotiator, as well as England's religious tolerance and economic strength as reasons for her effectiveness as a leader.

## CHAPTER 8

### BLACKLINE MASTER 1

1. Asia
2. the Indian Ocean
3. a sea route across the Atlantic Ocean and then an inland route to Tenochtitlán
4. Venice and Florence
5. about 900 miles; about 7,000 miles; about 7,000 miles

### BLACKLINE MASTER 2

1. *Possible answer:* He was impressed with the city and liked it. He uses words that have positive connotations and words such as *great, beautiful, very good,* and *pleasant* to describe details of the city.
2. He describes one square "with arcades all around, where more than sixty thousand people come each day to buy and sell, and where every kind of merchandise produced in these lands is found: provisions as well as ornaments of gold and silver, lead, brass, copper, tin, stones, shells, bones, and feathers."
3. "There are, in all districts of this great city, many temples."
4. *Possible answer:* Moctezuma's vassals were rich.

AN AGE OF VOYAGES, 1350–1600

# ANSWER KEY

## CHAPTER TEST
A. 1. a 2. c 3. b 4. c

B. 5. Students may cite opportunities such access to crafts and trade goods, theater, access to government and religious leaders, or the variety of activities available in cities.

6. Students may cite crime, poverty, disease, fire, or waste (or garbage)

C. Paragraphs will vary, but students should note several facts that the author uses to support the generalization. Students may mention the following: The world's first "shopping mall" was built in London in 1568. Merchants in Great Zimbabwe sold goods from India, Indonesia, and China. Florence had 277 shops of wool merchants, 83 warehouses belonging to silk merchants, and numerous craftspeople, such as cabinetmakers, stonecutters, goldsmiths, jewelers, grocers, and butchers, that produced goods. Venice had stores full of merchandise such as spices, rare cloths, and silk draperies. Weavers in Ahmedabad made fine cotton cloth, which was exported as far as Europe and China. In Tenochtitlán, a wide variety of provisions and ornaments were sold each day in the market square.

## CHAPTER 9
### BLACKLINE MASTER 1
1. They cover almost the same area, and spread from eastern Africa to the eastern coast of China.
2. about 6750 miles
3. Calicut
4. They would go overland through northern Egypt to the Red Sea, then sail down to the Arabian Sea and then down the coast of Africa to Mogadishu.
5. about 1800 miles.

### BLACKLINE MASTER 2
1. It would tell them how to get there and help them to estimate the length of their voyage, based on wind conditions. It would also give them directions to find the capital city.
2. It would probably encourage them, because it states that merchandise from all over the world is available at the marketplace, and everyone has enjoyed great profits.
3. It would tell them when pepper is available. It also advises them that a sales tax is required, and give them an estimate of the going price.
4. Yes, they probably did, since they gained the revenues from the sales taxes.

### CHAPTER TEST
A. 1. d 2. b 3. a 4. d

B. 5. Spices. Examples include pepper, cloves, nutmeg, mace, cardamom, cinnamon, and ginger. Spices were important to flavor and preserve food, but also as ingredients in perfumes, love potions, and painkillers.

6. Islamic law provided uniform standards for business practices. Therefore, no matter where they were trading, merchants could have the confidence that the procedures and rules would be familiar and standard.

7. He sponsored several voyages for exploration, trade, and colonization; he hired scholars to develop navigational tools; under his leadership, tiny Portugal developed into the European leader at sea.

C. Paragraphs should include the idea that all three were navigation tools. The compass indicated the directions of north, south, east, and west. The astrolabe helped them to observe and calculate the positions of planets and stars in the night sky. Since these positions were constants, captains could set their courses based on them. The astrolabe helped them to create astronomical charts, which showed the positions of stars and constellations in various seasons and locations.

## CHAPTER 10
### BLACKLINE MASTER 1
1. 1498
2. It was the most western European colony. Most likely he could stop there to get any needed supplies.
3. about 3,500 miles
4. about 100 miles per day
5. He explored it in 1498. During this expedition he discovered the mouth of a huge river and concluded that Venezuela was part of a continent.

### BLACKLINE MASTER 2
1. They did not have metal weapons.
2. He felt they were honest and free of deceit.
3. *Possible answer:* He respected them for not being lazy or awkward and because they had great knowledge of the seas; he showed a lack of respect by tricking them into exchanging valuable things for trifles.
4. *Possible answer:* They might have been impressed by the ability of the Spanish to sail across an ocean, easily conquer foreign people, and easily acquire their valuable goods.

### CHAPTER TEST
A. 1. c 2. d 3. b 4. a

B. 5. John Cabot landed in what is now Canada.

6. He received the financial support of Queen Isabella.

7. The Spanish and Portuguese realized that their expeditions might lead to disputes over land rights.

C. Students' paragraphs should explain that early mapmakers read and believed that Amerigo Vespucci was the first European to see what is now Venezuela. They popularized the name *America*, meaning "the land of Amerigo." By the time people realized that Columbus was the first European to arrive in this "new world," the name *America* was already in place.

## CHAPTER 11
### BLACKLINE MASTER 1
1. to North America, the Caribbean, and South America
2. the trip from Africa to North America
3. from the Caribbean and Brazil
4. *Possible answers:* to provide goods that were unavailable in Africa, to use as payments for slaves, for use in trading.
5. approximately 2,400 miles

### BLACKLINE MASTER 2
1. the King of Portugal, the captain of the ships, and the ships' crews
2. Sofala supplied the coast with cotton cloth, and it seems that the captain was allowed to claim most of it for himself.
3. *Possible answer:* It shows that the Portuguese domination of sea trade came from a history of violent, aggressive attacks in order to obtain goods and establish control.
4. The Chinese thought the Portuguese were rude and weak fighters. It is possible that the Chinese were far more prepared to fight the Portuguese than East African cities had been.

### CHAPTER TEST
A. 1. d 2. b 3. a 4. b

B. 5. *Possible answer:* Plantation owners treated their slaves as if they were machines that would eventually need replacement. However, slaves were also cruelly treated and punished by owners who saw them as property.

6. *Possible answer:* Catholic and Protestant churches did not oppose slavery outright, although some missionaries felt that slaves were mistreated.

C. *Possible answer:* Both endured difficult work and many dangers, but the lives of children who were slaves were far more harsh and brutal, because they were seen as property and less than human.

## CHAPTER 12
### BLACKLINE MASTER 1
1. Tenochtitlan and Acapulco
2. the Andes mountain range
3. It is close to the Pacific Ocean, and most large cities near bodies of water are port cities.
4. approx. 600 miles
5. *Possible answer:* Cuzco is in the Andes, so it was probably more difficult to reach.

# ANSWER KEY

## BLACKLINE MASTER 2
1. The writer views the siege as a tragedy, because of such phrases as "pity for the pain we suffered."
2. *Possible answer:* If you just read the Spanish point of view, you might think that the conquest was a good thing, because it brought wealth to Spain. Reading the Aztec point of view helps me understand the suffering they endured.
3. Many people were killed, the water was bad, the wells were blocked, there was little to eat.
4. They drank the water, even though it was bad; they ate wood, brackish food, chunks of adobe, lizards, vermin, dust, and worms.

## CHAPTER TEST
A. 1. a  2. d  3. d  4. a

B. 5. Many people throughout the Americas were killed or were weakened.

6. The Incas built roads throughout their empire.

7. The world population increased, despite the loss of life to disease.

C. Students' paragraphs should explain that mine owners were concerned that dangerous conditions at the mines and poisoning from the mercury, combined with diseases, had killed many workers. The Spaniards brought in some African slaves, but they died in great numbers. Then they tried new types of more efficient machinery. They eventually provided wages and better working conditions, although they still relied on slave labor.

## WRAP-UP TEST
1. Students' paragraphs should note that the Ottoman Empire's policy of religious tolerance meant that its people could practice the Muslim, Jewish, Christian, and other faiths. Trade and exploration led to mingling and blending of cultures among the people.
2. Students' main idea maps should note that cities along trade routes offered jobs and other opportunities. Jobs included providing food and supplies, places to stay, and forms of entertainment. Populations grew as people came for jobs. Larger populations created a need for even more jobs.
3. Paragraphs should mention that Zheng He's fleet carried huge amounts of cargo to the Philippines, the east coast of Africa, and the Arabian Peninsula. The voyages helped to make people of these areas aware of Chinese items such as silk and porcelain, and helped spur them to expand trade routes to China.
4. Paragraphs should include the idea that Prince Henry's explorers found a sea route around Africa, and that the voyagers returned with spices, gold, jewels, and other plunder that gave great trade wealth to Portugal. The wealth allowed Portugal to sponsor more voyages, and eventually led their exploration of Brazil in South America.
5. Venn diagrams should note that the Aztecs were conquered by Cortés in Mexico. The Incas were conquered by Pizarro in Peru. In both cases, the Spanish conquered an enemy weakened by hunger and disease. Both took advantage of local customs to attack an unsuspecting people. Both used local enemies of the Aztecs and Incas to enlarge their fighting force.
6. Students' paragraphs should cite effects such as the expense of luxury goods that had been transported along the Silk Road, and the rapid spread of the bubonic plague along the trade route.
7. Ferdinand and Isabella of Spain supported Columbus's first voyage, in part because they wanted to continue to spread their Catholic faith. Spain and Portugal both sought to spread their faith as they explored the New World. They had missionaries with them who attempted to convert people of the New World to the Catholic religion.
8. Ignatius Loyola founded the Jesuits as part of the reform of the Catholic Church following the Protestant Reformation. The Jesuits set up schools, taught at universities, preached, and worked as missionaries. In some areas they stopped the spread of Protestant ideas, and reconverted people who had left the church.
9. Map makers read and believed a letter written by Amerigo Vespucci, in which he claimed to be the first European to see what is now Venezuela. They printed the word "America" meaning "the land of Amerigo" on their maps of the New World, and the name stuck.
10. Students may choose to focus on the exchange of slaves, sugar, or manufactured goods. Charts should note impact on the society and economy of the time.

## ANSWERS FOR THE STUDENT STUDY GUIDE
## CHAPTER 1

### Access
Plague, Differences: contagious, caused by bacteria, began in 1333 in China and came back regularly during next 300 years, spread across Asia, Europe, and northern Africa, cause unknown during 14th century

Hundred Years' War, Differences: fought between England and France, started over rule of France, lasted from 1337 to 1453, took place in France, caused crops to be stolen, caused villages to be burned, in France, was paid for by taxes
Similarities: started in the 14th century, killed people and animals, caused misery, lowered population, which caused landlords to force fewer peasants to do more work, left fewer people to pay taxes and work, ignited revolts

### Cast of Characters
**Francesco Petrarch** was an Italian scholar and poet.
**Zhu Yuanzhang** founded the Ming dynasty in China.
**Giovanni Boccaccio** was a writer whose masterpiece was the *Decameron*, the introduction of which describes the effects of the plague on the city of Florence.

### What Happened When?
**1333:** The first outbreaks of the Black Death occurred.
**1368:** Zhu Yuanzhang led rebels to capture the Mongol capital city Khanbalik and founded the Ming dynasty.

### Word Bank
1. contagious  2. landlords  3. peasants  4. nobles  5. caravans

### Word Play
famine; Check students' sentences.

### Critical Thinking
1. c  2. d, f  3. a  4. b

### Working with Primary Sources: Identifying Point of View
1. The plague had killed many of his friends.
2. He compares life to a dream.
3. *Possible answer:* Life is lonely because so many of his friends have died. It is also like a bad dream or a nightmare, which is why he wishes he could have woken before it—a reaction people often have to bad dreams.
4. *Possible answer:* Life probably seemed unreal because the plague spread so quickly and killed so many people. The huge numbers of deaths caused by the plague probably seemed too fantastic and unreal, and thus were more fitting for a dream.

### All Over the Map
1. **a.** *Possible answer:* Go southeast from Khanbalik, then take a water route south through the South China Sea. Head northwest across the Indian Ocean, and go southwest around the peninsula of India. Then follow the pilgrim route to Mecca. **b.** about 6400 miles  **c.** Go southwest in a straight line from Khanbalik to Mecca. **d.** about 4800 miles  **e.** Plague might have reached Mecca earlier than it did because my route is shorter.
2. **a.** Follow the Silk Road to the northern tip of the Black Sea. Sail in a southwesterly direction across the Black Sea to the Mediterranean Sea. Then head in a northwesterly direction to Venice. **b.** about 6400 miles  **c.** Go northwest in a straight line from Khanbalik to Venice. **d.** about 6000 miles  e. Plague might have reached Venice earlier than it did because my route is shorter.

## CHAPTER 2

### Access
**What I Learned:** *Possible answers:* Italian cities grew wealthy and education known as humanism helped bring in a rebirth of thought.
Leonardo was an artist, inventor, and engineer.
Shakespeare used classical plots and humanist ideas, and studied people and their behavior.

### Cast of Characters
**Leonardo da Vinci:** Italian Renaissance artist, engineer, and inventor
**Lorenzo de' Medici:** wealthy merchant and ruler of Florence who supported humanism
**Francesco Petrarch:** Italian scholar, humanist, and poet
**Michelangelo Buonarotti:** Italian Renaissance artist, poet, and architect
**Niccolo Machiavelli:** author of The Prince
**Miguel de Cervantes:** Spanish author and playwright
**William Shakespeare:** English playwright and poet

### Word Bank
1. profit  2. theories  3. diplomats  4. material world  5. moral code  6. romantic

### Word Play
self-portraits, three dimensions; Check students' sentences.

### Critical Thinking
**Detail:** Italian merchants grew wealthy from trade and came to control their cities.
**Detail:** Their financial success provided money to spend on luxuries like art and music.
**Detail:** They supported education and helped spread the ideas of humanism.
**Detail:** They supported and hired artists.

**AN AGE OF VOYAGES, 1350–1600**

# ANSWER KEY

### Working with Primary Sources
1. He seems to be praising many human abilities and gifts.
2. Hamlet praises all that humans can do and aspire to; he details how humans are unique and close to God. These ideas can also be seen in the works and writings of many Renaissance artists and writers, such as Petrarch, Leonardo, and Michelangelo.
3. *Possible answer:* Shakespeare had a sense of humor and irony, and enjoyed poking fun at human vanity.

### All Over the Map
Check students' maps for accuracy.

## CHAPTER 3

### Access
**Detail:** Confucian ideas became the core of Chinese culture.
**Detail:** Society became a well-ordered hierarchy.
**Detail:** Scholar-officials—both noble and commoners—studied Confucian philosophy, law, and literature.
**Detail:** Neo-Confucians believed the best life was one of service.
**Detail:** Ming leaders were expected to solve practical problems, such as strengthening the Great Wall.
**Detail:** Emperor Yongle supported the arts and exploration.
**Detail:** Spanish and Portuguese merchants brought new crops to China, which helped its growing population.
**Detail:** Wealthy people in China and other civilizations purchased Chinese porcelain and lacquerware.
**Detail:** Scholar-officials created paintings, wrote poetry in calligraphy, and produced philosophy, poetry, or history that would teach moral lessons.
**Detail:** Writers produced works for enjoyment, such as *The Golden Lotus* and *The Monkey King*.

### Cast of Characters
**Hongwu** founded the Ming dynasty in China.
**Tang Xianzu** was a Chinese playwright who wrote *The Peony Pavilion*.
**Wang Yangming** was a neo-Confucian scholar.
As emperor, **Yongle** sent naval expeditions to the Indian Ocean.

### What Happened When
**1368:** the start of the Ming dynasty
**1644:** the collapse of the Ming dynasty
**Math Challenge:** 276 years

### Word Bank
1. *Possible answer:* After Hongwu defeated the warlords, he set up the Ming dynasty.
2. *Possible answer:* According to Confucian ideas, society should be organized as a hierarchy.
3. *Possible answer:* Scholar-officials studied the past to develop the ideas of neo-Confucianism.

### Word Play
Students' advertisements should describe porcelain as strong, delicate, blue-and-white dishes or vases. They should describe lacquerware as durable, waterproof items usually made of wood and coated with many layers of varnish.

### Critical Thinking
**Hongwu's Rule:** defeated Mongols; began the Ming dynasty
**Similarities:** Ming emperor; absolute rule; society based on hierarchy; supported Confucian ideas; supported scholarship
**Yongle's Rule:** came to power through violent overthrow of nephew; supported exploration and trade with outsiders

### Drawing Conclusions
1. It describes Wang Zhen as working hard to support his family and living frugally. It states that he organized famine relief measures to help the larger society.
2. wasteful
3. It is a tribute to the person, most likely paid by his family. It would not include negative qualities.
4. Perhaps he sold valuable Chinese goods, such as porcelain or lacquerware.

### All Over the Map
Be sure students can explain the placement of arrows and icons on the map.

## CHAPTER 4

### Access
**Detail:** How did the press work? Type was set with individual letters, which could be used over and over again.
**Detail:** Who worked in print shops? Master printers, apprentices, journeymen
**Detail:** What was printed? Anything that would sell; books on law, medicine, grammar, prayers, Bibles, and saints' lives
**Detail:** What changes occurred? Books became cheaper; new jobs became available; mass culture was established; people could collaborate and share ideas on all topics.

### Cast of Characters
**Johan Gutenberg:** German goldsmith who invented the printing press with movable type

### Word Bank
1. movable type  2. copyright  3. professionals  4. apprentice  5. mass culture

### Word Play
craft guild; Check students' sentences.

### Critical Thinking
1. b  2. d.  3. a  4. f.  5. e

### Making Inferences
1. Women of her time were not formally trained in most trades; it was unusual that she was involved in publishing.
2. "it is not unheard of"
3. Women were probably successful; she says that women received "the highest of praise."
4. Since she was involved in publishing, her words probably appeared in a book.
5. *Possible answers:* Yes. She may have had to learn her skills more quickly, or from her husband, since she had not been trained as an apprentice or journeyman. If it was unusual for women to be involved in publishing, she may have faced discrimination.

### All Over the Map
Check students' maps and legends. Students' maps should include the following icons: China: Woodblock printing; may have invented paper; Korea: Woodblock printing; movable ceramic, wooden, and metal type

## CHAPTER 5

### Access
**Effect**
1. They began to criticize the church.
2. Their ideas became widespread.
3. They supported the idea that the church should not have special privileges.
4. Denmark, Sweden, Norway, England, Poland, and territories within the German empire became Protestant.
5. Many thousands were persecuted, tortured, and executed; many others migrated.
6. Calvinist teachings appealed to many people, such as merchants.
7. They stopped the spread of Protestantism in some places.
8. Religious wars broke out in Europe.

### Cast of Characters
**Ignatius Loyola:** a Spanish Catholic who founded the Jesuits.
**John Calvin:** a French Protestant religious reformer.
**Desiderius Erasmus:** a Dutch humanist, scholar, and author.
**Martin Luther:** a German monk who began the Protestant Reformation.
**William Tyndale:** an English religious reformer.

### Word Bank
1. pacifist  2. inquisition  3. missionary  4. persecution  5. Protestant Reformation

### Word Play
*Possible answer:* The pope decreed that Martin Luther was a heretic who went against church teachings.

### Critical Thinking
Students should draw a sound conclusion about how the Catholic Reformation revitalized the Catholic Church. Their paragraph should describe what they read, what they know, and their conclusion. Topics might include the work of the Jesuits or the Council of Trent.

# ANSWER KEY

### Identifying Point of View
1. He compares the lowliness of man with the greatness of God.
2. He might criticize the bishop for not living simply and humbly.
3. You can tell that he has strong beliefs about the strength and power of God.
4. *Possible answer:* Perhaps his experience as a lawyer had exposed him to criminals and others who had done things he could not approve of. It may also have seemed logical to him that God was superior to humans God had created.

### All Over the Map
Be sure students can explain the placement of icons, arrows, and dates on the map.

## CHAPTER 6

### Access
*Possible answers*, the Ottoman Empire:
- constructed many mosques
- used Janissaries to expand troops and strengthen Muslim control
- controlled parts of Europe and Asia

*Possible answers*, the Mughal Empire
- grew to its greatest size under the emperor Akbar
- brought other religions to the empire and developed new ones within
- established the Divine Faith, with Akbar at its center

*Possible answers*, Similarities
- was a gunpowder empire
- promoted learning and the arts
- expanded during the 16th century

### Cast of Characters
**Suleyman:** sultan of the Ottoman Empire
**Isabella of Castile:** queen of Spain
**Ferdinand of Aragon:** king of Spain
**Selim "the Grim":** Ottoman sultan, father of Suleiman
**Akbar:** Mughal emperor and religious reformer
**Babur:** founder of the Mughal Empire, grandfather of Akbar

### What Happened When?
**1345:** Ottoman forces entered Europe.
**1469:** Isabella married Ferdinand.
**1492:** Ferdinand and Isabella's armies conquered Granada; the rulers orders all Jews to leave Spain

### Word Bank
1. tolerance  2. bureaucracy  3. religious diversity  4. convert  5. hostile

### Word Play
scapegoats; Check students' sentences.

### Critical Thinking
*Possible answer:* Akbar appointed both Muslims and Hindus to help run his kingdom, and he allowed people to follow their own religious beliefs. This helped him strengthen his kingdom and bring his people together.

### Compare and Contrast
1. *Possible answer:* He seems to think Isabella is quite beautiful and worthy of respect, but I am not sure whether he admires her as a person.
2. *Possible answer:* She seems to have been a self-controlled and controlling person. She commanded respect through her words and her actions.
3. *Possible answer:* I don't think she changed dramatically. From the early description, she seems beautiful with a tendency to be harsh, and the second excerpt makes that quality even clearer.

### All Over the Map
Check students' maps for accuracy.

## CHAPTER 7

### Access
**Main Idea:** Elizabeth I never let being a woman stand in the way of being an effective ruler.
  **Detail:** She was an excellent negotiator, and used her language skills to get what she wanted.
  **Detail:** She helped England avoid bankruptcy by bringing in taxes with her support of the wool trade, and by keeping the country out of war as much as possible.
  **Detail:** She brought religious peace by allowing some diversity.

**Main Idea:** Sunni Ali Ber built the Songhay Empire in western Africa.
  **Detail:** He conquered neighboring territory.
  **Detail:** He appointed officials to oversee his territory.
  **Detail:** He increased the size of the army, and provided training for soldiers.
**Main Idea:** Under Askia the Great, the Songhay Empire became the largest and wealthiest kingdom in western Africa.
  **Detail:** He used Islam to help unify his kingdom.
  **Detail:** He divided his empire into well-governed provinces.
  **Detail:** He encouraged trade to increase the amount of money in the royal treasury.
**Main Idea:** Afonso I's reign included both prosperity and weakness.
  **Detail:** He built many churches, and encouraged trade.
  **Detail:** He tried to put a stop to the slave trade.
  **Detail:** The slave trade depopulated his kingdom and led to its breakup.

### Cast of Characters
**Elizabeth I:** queen of England during a time of prosperity
**Sunni Ali Ber:** ruler who built the Songhay Empire
**Askia the Great:** ruler who increased the size and wealth of the Songhay Empire
**Afonso I:** ruler of the Kingdom of Kongo

### Word Bank
1. monarch  2. negotiations  3. mosques  4. diplomacy  5. commerce

### Word Play
traditional; Check students' sentences.

### Identifying Point of View
1. crooked leg, bleary eye  2. She may have meant someone who was deceitful, or not trusting.  3. She thought such a person was uglier than someone with physical deformities.  4. The suspicion and lack of trust she had witnessed in her father and half-sister's actions.

### All Over the Map
Be sure students can explain the routes they suggest and choose.

## CHAPTER 8

### Access
**Main Idea:** Cities offered people various job opportunities.
  **Detail:** People worked as merchants or shopkeepers.
  **Detail:** People produced goods; for example, working as cabinetmakers, stonecutters, goldsmiths, or jewelers.
  **Detail:** People were officials or bureaucrats.
  **Detail:** People worked for the Church
  **Detail:** People worked as laborers, digging ditches or hauling goods
**Main Idea:** Cities had many problems.
  **Detail:** Diseases spread easily in crowded conditions.
  **Detail:** Fire spread easily.
  **Detail:** Crime was common.
  **Detail:** Poverty was a problem.
  **Detail:** Trash and waste made cities smell.

### Cast of Characters
**Hernán Cortés** was a Spanish explorer and military leader who conquered the Aztec Empire in 1521.
**Moctezuma II** was an Aztec emperor.

### What Happened When?
**1521** Hernán Cortés conquered the Aztec Empire.
**1666** The Great Fire of London destroyed more than 13,000 homes and nearly 100 churches

### Word Bank
1. bishops  2. capital  3. immigrants  4. servants  5. council  6. slaves  7. prophecy

### Word Play
bureaucrats; Check students' sentences.

# ANSWER KEY

### Make Generalizations
1. Facts that support the generalization: London was a capital. So were Istanbul, Paris, Rome, Beijing, and Ahmedabad.

    The generalization appears accurate because the author mentions many large cities that were also capitals.

2. Facts that support the generalization: In London, people could go to plays and bearbaitings; tour buildings such as Westminster Abbey, Whitehall Palace, and the Tower of London; watch trials and executions; and listen to music. Men could gather in public places for conversation or share food and beverages in tearooms, coffeehouses, or taverns. People could go shopping in cities such as London, Great Zimbabwe, Istanbul, Florence, Venice, and Tenochtitlán. People worked as shopkeepers or merchants in London, Great Zimbabwe, Istanbul, Florence, Venice, Antwerp, Ahmedabad, Beijing, and Tenochtitlán. People worked as weavers in Ahmedabad. Officials, nobles, lawyers, and bureaucrats worked in capital cities, such as London, Istanbul, Paris, and Rome. The pope and bishops also worked in Rome. Servants, cooks, and officials worked in Beijing. Laborers and messengers worked in Beijing and in London. People hauled away trash in Tenochtitlán. Women in London might work as waitresses, musicians, and actresses.

    The generalization appears accurate because the author includes numerous examples of specific leisure activities and jobs in several cities.

3. "Along with work and leisure, worship was also an important activity in cities."

    Facts that support the generalization: Baron Waldstein visited St. Paul's and other churches in London, as well as the royal chapels in Westminster Abbey. Visitors to Rome, Istanbul, Ahmedabad, and Tenochtitlán commented on the cities' religious buildings, some of which were crowded with worshippers, altars, and artwork. The pope, who was the head of the Catholic Church, ruled Rome. Ahmedabad was filled with mosques. Tenochtitlán had a huge religious center with many temples, and Cortés specified that all districts of Tenochtitlán had many temples. Beijing had temples built in many different architectural styles.

    The generalization appears accurate because the author mentions specific cities that had numerous examples of places to worship, mentions a city (Rome) that had a religious leader as its ruler, and mentions that visitors to several cities commented on the crowds of worshippers in religious buildings.

### Working with Primary Sources
1. its great wealth
2. stored for future needs
3. in the churches
4. He wanted the great wealth of the city.

### Compare and Contrast
Both describe the cities' wealth. Guicciardini focuses on the actions of the people while Mehmed I talks about homes and buildings.

### All Over the Map
Students' map keys should have different icons for beads, cloth, porcelain, and fine cotton cloth. Arrows on their maps should show cloth and beads coming from Indonesia and India and going to Great Zimbabwe, porcelain coming from China and going to Great Zimbabwe, and fine cotton cloth going from Ahmedabad toward Beijing (China) and Europe. Map titles may vary but should explain what the map shows.

## CHAPTER 9

### Access
2. Effect: The Chinese destroyed Zheng He's maps so no more voyages would be attempted. 3. Effect: Sea routes became popular. 5. Cause: Chinese silk was very expensive. 6. Cause: Portuguese captains wanted to find a sea route to the Indian Ocean. 7. Effect: Many European rulers were eager to send their own voyages of exploration.

### Cast of Characters
**Zheng He:** Chinese admiral who headed naval expeditions to the Indian Ocean

**Henry "the Navigator":** Portuguese prince who supported voyages of exploration and trade

**Bartolomeu Dias:** Portuguese sea captain who first rounded the southern tip of Africa

**Vasco da Gama:** Portuguese sea captain who first reached India by sailing around the southern tip of Africa

### Word Bank
**1198**: Innocent III became pope

**1215**: Frederick II became king of Germany; Magna Carta was signed; Lateran Council convened

**1250**: Frederick II died

**1282**: Peter of Aragon took control of Sicily

### Word Bank
1. cosmopolitan 2. luxury goods 3. fleet 4. astronomical charts 5. emperor 6. admiral 7. merchant

### Word Play
Check students' sentences.

### Critical Thinking
1. **land routes:** required horses, camels, or other beasts of burden; expensive and dangerous; often in disrepair

    **both:** connected nations; often quite profitable; helped trading cities grow and prosper

    **sea routes:** required ships; brought new technologies; led to exploration, discovery, and colonization; less expensive and dangerous than land routes

2. **sakk:** Arabian word; a letter that proved money was deposited in another city; people collected funds from the business that held the merchant's money

    **both:** more secure than cash; eliminated need to carry a lot of cash

    **modern bank check:** issued by a bank; people deposit money in bank and then draw it out by writing checks; banks collect the funds from the issuing bank

3. **Bartolomeu Dias:** first to round tip of Africa; forced to return to Portugal by tired seamen

    **both:** 15th-century Portuguese sea captains who rounded the tip of Africa

    **Vasco da Gama:** first to round the tip of Africa, explore the east coast, and reach India; conquered the Indian city of Calicut; made three voyages in all; was highly successful

### What Happened When?
**1405:** Zheng He's first voyage

**1488:** Dias rounds the tip of Africa.

**1497:** da Gama finds a sea route to India

Check students' timelines for accuracy.

### Drawing Conclusions/Identifying Point of View
1. *Possible answer:* The writer may have been an officer of da Gama's, or a historian sent on the voyage to record events. He was important enough to have accompanied da Gama to a meeting with the king.
2. *Possible answer:* The king probably expected gifts from anyone who visited his kingdom.
3. *Possible answer:* The king expects gifts that are of comparable value to those he will give to the visitors. He is aware of what da Gama is likely to have available for trade.
4. The "scarlet cloth" is probably silk.
5. *Possible answer:* The king understands that da Gama intends to trade to gain wealth, and that the spices and other riches of his kingdom are of value to da Gama.
6. *Possible answer:* The formal language the writer used shows that he was somewhat impressed by the king, and by the riches of the kingdom.

### All Over the Map
**A. Route 2:** Sail south from Portugal along the western coast of Africa, around the tip, and then sail north up the eastern coast of Africa to Mombasa. Distance traveled: about 7500 miles.

**B. Route 1:** Take the overland route west, along the Silk Road. Once in Persia, turn south on the overland route and continue south to India. Continue traveling along the western coast of India to Calicut. Distance traveled: about 4500 miles.

**Route 2:** Sail south along the coast of China in the East China Sea to the South China Sea. Continue sailing south until you reach Malacca. Then sail west across the Indian Ocean to India, and north along the western coast of India to Calicut. Distance traveled: about 3400 miles.

## CHAPTER 10

### Access
**What I Learned:** He used the knowledge of sailors and studied ancient texts from Egypt and Greece.

**What I Learned:** He captured some of them and proclaimed that their land belonged to Spain.

**What I Learned:** It was a difficult journey. Most of the sailors died, and only one of the ships made it back to Spain.

# ANSWER KEY

### Cast of Characters
**Christopher Columbus:** He was the first European since the Vikings to cross the Atlantic.
**Henry "the Navigator":** He was the Portuguese prince who supported voyages of exploration and trade.
**John Cabot:** He headed the first English expedition to North America
**Amerigo Vespucci:** He was an Italian explorer whose name was given to the Americas.
**Bartolomeu Dias:** He was a Portuguese captain who first rounded the southern tip of Africa.
**Pedro Alvares Cabral:** He was a Portuguese adventurer who first landed in what is now Brazil.

### Word Bank
1. caravel 2. mariners 3. astrolabe 4. colony 5. lateen sail

### Word Play
Students' sentences should state that Vikings used sagas to tell their history.

### Critical Thinking
Students should list two related facts about colonization or another topic from the chapter and write a sound generalization based on the facts.

### What Happened When?
**1492:** Columbus's first voyage
**1493:** Columbus's second voyage
**1497:** first English voyage to North America
**1498:** Columbus's third voyage
**1500:** Dias and Cabral discover Brazil
**1502:** Columbus's fourth voyage

### Identifying Point of View
1. forests, salmon
2. He or she might have felt there were more opportunities in Canada than in icy Greenland.
3. *Possible answer:* They could study forests in Canada to determine what they might have been like when the sagas were first told.
4. *Possible answer:* It might be difficult to verify that the salmon were bigger than they had ever seen before.

### All Over the Map
Students' five questions should show an understanding of how to use latitude and longitude, and they should apply to the map of Columbus's voyages. They should answer their partners' questions correctly.

## CHAPTER 11

### Access
*Possible answers:*
**Detail:** Sailors could be violent and cruel.
**Detail:** Sea voyages were physically unpleasant.
**Detail:** Malnutrition and disease were common and often fatal.
**Detail:** Sailors were separated from their families for long periods of time.

### Cast of Characters
*Possible answer:* Amerigo Vespucci described the hammock, which was used late in the 16th century for sleeping on ships. Before then, crews slept uncomfortably on deck.

### What Happened When?
Spain controlled Portugal during that time, and as a result, the flow of silver and other goods to and from America and Europe and Asia was easier.

### Word Bank
1. dominate 2. malnutrition 3. plantations 4. cultivation 5. contract 6. refining 7. racist

### Word Play
The Greek words *mono* and *tone* make up *monotonous*; thinking about a repeated sound heard over and over helps one understand that *monotonous* can mean dull and repetitious.

### Critical Thinking
1. The Chinese clearly had little respect for the Portuguese. It is unlikely that they would want to become trading partners with them.
2. The Chinese thought that Portuguese ships were safe, but their point of view about Portuguese sailors probably did not change very much.

### Working with Primary Sources
1. assaulted, fiercely, captured
2. examined, approved, marked
3. *Possible answer:* Bosman's tone is unemotional and somewhat medical, while Hawkins' tone is more aggressive. The quotations are similar, however, in the horrors they describe and in their complete lack of caring and compassion towards Africans.

### All Over the Map
Check students' maps for accuracy.

## CHAPTER 12

### Access
**Differences (Conquest of the Aztec Empire):** led by Hernán Cortés; took place in Tenochtitlan, in what is now Mexico, in 1519; Aztec Empire much smaller than Inca Empire
**Similarities:** European diseases killed and weakened many native people. Local allies supported the Spanish conquerors. The Spanish conquerors had guns. The Spanish founded new towns, built Christian churches, and set up agricultural plantations. The Spanish discovered silver mines.
**Differences (Conquest of the Inca Empire):** led by Francisco Pizarro; took place in Cuzco, in what is now Peru, in 1533; Inca Empire much larger than Aztec Empire

### Cast of Characters
*Possible answer:* Hernán Cortés defeated the Aztec emperor Moctezuma II.
*Possible answer:* After the death of Atahualpa, Francisco Pizarro was able to conquer the Inca Empire.

### What Happened When?
**1519:** Cortés went to Mexico in search of gold.
**1521:** Cortés took control of Aztec Empire.
**1533:** Pizarro took control of the Inca Empire.

### Word Bank
1. missions 2. revenue 3. epidemic 4. baroque 5. allies 6. mestizos 7. tributes

### Word Play
The word *conquer* comes from the Latin word *conquīrere*, which means "to procure."

### Critical Thinking
1. As a result, they could more easily convert native people to Christianity.
2. As a result, European men entered into relationships with native or slave women, and a mestizo society developed.
3. As a result, the demand for products with caffeine grew.
4. As a result, there were disagreements among the ruling elite about who should be the next emperor.

### Identifying Point of View
1. He feels sorry for them. He calls them "poor fellows" and describes their difficult working conditions.
2. He might not have liked it, because it is critical of the mine owners.
3. It was made during the time when Europe had colonies in the Americas and exported goods for their profits.
4. Many workers were hired to work in the mines. They had primitive equipment. They worked very hard, in dangerous conditions.

### All Over the Map
Students should be able to explain the exchange of people and goods into and out of the Americas.

AN AGE OF VOYAGES, 1350–1600

www.ingramcontent.com/pod-product-compliance
Lightning Source LLC
LaVergne TN
LVHW080250260326
834688LV00042BA/1204

*9 780195 223446*